THE WAY OF A DISCIPLE

WALKING WITH JESUS

The Walking with God Series

VOLUME 1

DON COUSINS AND JUDSON POLING

CONTENTS

PREFACE

The *Walking with God Series* was developed as the core curriculum for small groups at Willow Creek Community Church in South Barrington, Illinois. The material here flows out of the vision and values of this dynamic and world-renowned ministry. In the early years of Willow Creek, small groups using these studies produced many of the leaders, both staff and volunteer, throughout the church.

Don Cousins, who at the time was associate pastor at Willow Creek, wrote the first draft of this material and used it with his own small group. After testing it there, he revised it and passed his notes to Judson Poling, who was the director of curriculum development. Judson edited and expanded the outlines, and then several pilot groups helped retool the material. After the pilot groups completed the studies, a team of leaders labored through a yearlong, line-by-line revision. The revisions became the original six-volume *Walking with God Series*. Since its first publication in 1992, the series has sold more than one million copies and has been translated into seven languages.

Thirty years later, the authors have reworked the six-book series and created this updated and condensed edition, now 42 sessions in two volumes (instead of 78 sessions in six books). However, while there are fewer sessions overall, the authors have made sure this adaptation is true to the original and retains the distinctives of that proven study. They believe this new version will reach a whole new generation of Christ-followers who seek to become mature disciples of Jesus. A small group that uses and completes *The Way of a Disciple: Walking with Jesus* and *The Work of a Disciple: Living Like Jesus* will lay a solid foundation for a lifelong walk with God.

PART 1

DEVELOPING INTIMACY WITH GOD

At its core, Christianity is Christ. Christians embrace a Person, not merely a philosophy. It is not so much knowing about his teaching as it is about knowing him. The greatest misunderstanding about Christianity today, even in the church, is the perception that God's bottom-line requirements are deeds to be done and beliefs to be believed. The Christ who spoke is bypassed for the things he spoke; the Guide is left behind for the guidance; the Commander is ignored for the carrying out of commands.

This series addresses the problem by encouraging Christians to develop a relationship with the living God. We believe that mature discipleship encompasses four foundational practices. A disciple of Jesus Christ is one who . . .

- Walks with God
- Lives the Word
- Contributes to the work of Christ
- Impacts the world

The two volumes in this series will encourage these four activities in the life of a believer. This volume, *The Way of a Disciple*, begins with a study of that essential relationship between you and God ("Developing Intimacy with God"). The next two parts examine the life of Jesus ("Getting to Know Jesus" and "Following Jesus"). The next volume, *The Work of a Disciple*, discusses your place in the gathering of believers known as the church ("Life-Changing Community" and "Building Your Church"). The study concludes by discussing ways you can make your mark for God's kingdom ("Making a Difference in Your World").

We do not intend to bury people in mountains of theological information. Our interest is in transforming hearts. We would readily recommend two years of a small-group experience that truly caused people to know God over twenty years of "Christian education" that rendered them all but dead to the real world and the God who is willing to walk with them in it. Group discussions alone won't produce that change. Thus, we have designed the weekly assignments as a systematic way of getting people to begin their own times alone with God—a practice we believe (and objective data shows) leads to deep and lasting transformation.*

Here is probably the best way to measure success for all who use this series: *How consistently do you walk with God after the study is over?*

---

* See Greg Hawkins and Cally Parkinson, *Move: What 1,000 Churches REVEAL about Spiritual Growth* (Grand Rapids: Zondervan, 2011).

A FRIEND WORTH HAVING

PERSONAL STUDY: John 1–3; 1 John 1–2
SCRIPTURE MEMORY: Revelation 3:20; 1 John 5:13
ON YOUR OWN: What Is God Like?

"What comes into our minds when we think about God is the most important thing about us."
—A. W. TOZER

What Is Your View of God?

Suppose you have to choose between two people who want to go to dinner with you. The first person is very warm and takes a genuine interest in others. He listens attentively and is fun to be with. Those who develop a friendship with him want it to last a lifetime.

In contrast, the second person is aloof and demanding. He keeps most of his friends (if you could call them that) at a distance. The only time he calls you is when he wants something from you. He's pretty unpredictable emotionally, and you never quite know where you stand with him. He wields considerable influence, but if it weren't for his power, he probably wouldn't have any friends at all.

You'd rather have dinner with the first person, right?

Now think about your image of God. Which is he more like—the first person or the second? Unfortunately, many people have a distorted view of God's character. To them, he's a divine version of the second person—distant and uncaring. Although he is powerful, they can't count on him. The only real benefit in knowing him comes from occasional answers to prayer. No wonder people have a hard time relating to God! Who would want to cultivate a friendship like that?

If your view of God has been colored by mistaken assumptions and erroneous ideas, it can be startling to learn that God longs to establish a close, intimate friendship with you. This study will help you understand what it means to relate to God in a personal way and how you can be assured of your eternal destiny. Let this one truth sink in: *God is a Friend worth having.*

1. What are some necessary ingredients for building a relationship with another person?

2. How do these compare with what you think might be necessary ingredients for cultivating a relationship with God?

Why You Can Have a Personal Relationship with God

3. *God has chosen you.* Why is it significant that Jesus said, "I chose you" (John 15:16)?

4. *God wants to spend time with you.* What does it mean when Jesus says that he wants to eat with you (see Revelation 3:20)?

5. *God will never leave you.* How do you respond to the promise that God will never leave you (see Hebrews 13:5)?

What God Has Given You to Establish This Relationship

6. *He gave you his Son.* What did God accomplish through giving his Son (see John 3:16)?

7. *He gave you a book.* Why is the Bible so important for your relationship with God (see Matthew 4:4)?

8. *He gave you his Spirit.* What does the Holy Spirit do for you (see John 16:13–14)?

How to Be Sure You're a Christian

No couple can build a lasting marriage if one partner is unsure of the love of the other. What if a spouse isn't even sure if the other person accepts him or her completely and doubts the other's commitment for life? A marriage with that degree of uncertainty is unstable and unhealthy.

The same is true in our relationship with God. People who aren't sure of their salvation can never fully experience the blessing of their union with Christ. On the other hand, there are people who assume they will go to heaven while failing to ask what might still stand in the way. These people may live with false hope and may possibly face eternal destruction.

When it comes to assurance of salvation, people fall into three categories: (1) those who live with confidence that they have salvation; (2) those who at times doubt their salvation; and (3) those who hope they are forgiven but lack assurance.

False Assurances of Salvation

Examine the following assumptions. I'm assured of salvation because . . .

- I believe there is a God.
- I'm basically a good person.
- I attend church and pray often.
- I was baptized or confirmed.
- I once prayed a prayer and asked God into my heart.

9. *"I believe there is a God."* How can a person believe in God and yet not have salvation?

10. *"I'm basically a good person."* Why is trusting one's own goodness a false basis for being included in God's kingdom?

11. *"I attend church and pray often."* Why doesn't being religious give enough assurance of salvation?

12. *"I was baptized or confirmed."* Why could a person have been baptized yet not have assurance of salvation?

13. *"I once prayed a prayer and asked God into my heart."* How could a person invite God into his or her heart and still not have a relationship with God?

Genuine Assurance of Salvation

14. *Read John 1:12.* According to this verse, what do we do?

15. According to this verse, what does God do?

16. *Read John 5:24.* According to this verse, what do we do?

17. According to this verse, what does God do?

Tests for Those Who Want to Be Sure

18. *The repentance test.* What does it mean for a person to repent (see Acts 3:19)?

19. *The presence test.* What does the Holy Spirit do for a believer (see Romans 8:15–16)?

20. *The evidence test.* What will be true of someone who has an authentic relationship with Christ (see 1 John 2:3–6)?

Apply It to Your Life

21. *Read 1 John 5:11–13.* The phrase "that you may know" implies a strong level of certainty. Why might God want you to be *sure* that you possess eternal life?

Your Walk with God

Central to the values behind this series is the belief that regular appointments with God will serve your spiritual life better in the long run than doing fill-in-the-blank "homework" related to the small-group study. Therefore, in this curriculum, your walk with God *is* the homework. Considering the pace of modern life, we thought it impractical for the average person to complete lengthy assignments to prepare for group meetings *and* have quiet times. For this reason, the material in this section was designed to help you establish simple foundational practices to enable you to maintain a vital connection with God.

Bible

Schedule three times this week to be alone with God. Pick the time during the day that works best for you. Each day, read the passage indicated below, write down one idea for application, and make a list of what you learn about Jesus from your study. Also, read over the article in the *On Your Own* section that follows.

DAY ONE: JOHN 1:1–2:12

Some of the things I observe in this passage:

One idea for how to apply this passage to my life:

DAY TWO: JOHN 2:14–3:36

Some of the things I observe in this passage:

One idea for how to apply this passage to my life:

DAY THREE: 1 JOHN 1–2

Some of the things I observe in this passage:

One idea for how to apply this passage to my life:

Prayer

Spend a few minutes praying about things that come to mind during your Bible reading. Also, identify something for which you can be thankful. At the end of the week, list two or three benefits you received from these appointments with God.

Scripture Memory

As part of the curriculum, we've included memory verses with each study. If you desire to make this discipline part of your discipleship experience, begin by memorizing these verses:

> *Here I am! I stand at the door and knock. If anyone hears my voice and opens the door, I will come in and eat with that person, and they with me* (Revelation 3:20).

> *I write these things to you who believe in the name of the Son of God so that you may know that you have eternal life* (1 John 5:13).

Next time, we will begin a lesson on the value of personal Bible study, the difference between *reading* the Bible and *studying* it, and the importance of memorizing Scripture. If you want to prepare for the study, think about different ways you can get the teachings of the Bible into your life. Then consider why the Bible is important and what it does for you.

On Your Own: What Is God Like?

Most people think they know the answer to that question. It wouldn't even occur to them that they might not have an accurate picture of God. "Everybody knows what God is like! He's, uh . . . well, he's . . ." What follows is a mishmash of ideas people have heard from parents and teachers over the years—ideas never critically examined but firmly believed. At an even deeper level, what people *feel* toward God flows out of their life experiences—and is equally subjective and untested.

- My grandma talked about God, and she was very nice to me—I guess I see God like her.
- I grew up in a very strict home with lots of rules—pretty much like God treats me now.
- Most ministers say God loves me—I guess he's like that.
- Most ministers say God is really mad at me—I guess he's like that.

Let's begin with this assumption: some of our perspectives about God are wrong. We've seen too much, been hurt too much, and been confused too much to assert we've got an accurate picture of God in every area. Somehow, we got some misinformation—every one of us. So we'll either have to take deliberate steps to reeducate ourselves about what he's like, or our view of him will continue to be out of focus . . . and will probably get worse with time.

Getting an Accurate Picture

Where do we begin to get an accurate picture? A good place to start is with what God has done. By seeing his acts, we can get a picture of the one responsible for them. Just as art tells us something about the artist, or a person's work tells us about his or her abilities and interests, what God has created tells us about what he, the Creator, is like.

As we look at creation—nature, the world, the stars and planets—one undeniable conclusion emerges: the one responsible for all this must be powerful beyond comparison. From the tiniest single-cell amoeba to entire distant galaxies racing away at unimaginable speeds, from an intricately complex snowflake to a sunset that sends amber blasts of color across the expansive sky, God's handiwork is so evident that we actively have to suppress what we see and feel in order to ignore him.

Yet the Bible tells us that is exactly what we do (see Romans 1:18–20). That inner sense of his majesty—clearly evident in the cosmos—is squelched. We hear the Voice . . . and ignore it. And so, while we all carry around some sense of his grandeur, we've modified our image of him until the gap between who we perceive him to be and who he really is becomes uncrossable. Sin—our deliberate attempts to expel him from the throne of the universe and our passive indifference to his rule—not only messes up our lives but also our view of God.

But our condition is not hopeless. God doesn't just *do*—he *speaks*. He talks to us. He sends messages. He tells us the truth through prophets and leaders. The Bible is the written record of his love. We learn things from this book that we couldn't know otherwise.

What We Learn from the Bible

For one thing, we learn that we need to cultivate and expand the sense of awe we get from his creation. Every notion we have of his power is true—and then some. But we also learn that his power is restrained. He isn't an angry father about to blow his cool. He's a loving Father desiring to be close to us.

In the earliest parts of the Bible, we see God calling out a single man, Abraham, for a special purpose: to make a nation that would represent God to the world. That group of people was intended to be a tangible picture of his love, power, justice, and holiness. They'd be different from the rest of the world—because he is different. They'd be holy—because he is holy. They'd show compassion—because he is compassionate. They'd avoid sin—because he has no sin. They'd be blessed—because it is his nature to bless. Next to the picture of God painted in creation would be this picture painted through a unique group of people. He would talk *to* them and talk to the rest of the world *through* them.

But God didn't just *do* and didn't just *speak*. He *became*. His work ordered the nothingness and made it a world for all to see. His words came to the prophets and apostles and made a book for all to read. His Word came to dwell among us in Jesus for all to receive. We *see* his handiwork; we *read* his book; we *meet* his Son. Jesus is the ultimate picture of God—the work, words, and Word of God incarnate. What Jesus does, God does. What he loves, God loves. What he hates, God hates. What he says, God says. How he acts, God acts.

Look no further for clarification of what God is like: the only begotten Son has fully explained him (see John 1:18). He showed God's awesome power by stilling the storm, healing the sick, and raising the dead—creation was subject to him. He showed God's desire to speak to us by unsurpassed teaching—truth was fully represented by him. And he lived out God's compassion without compromising his righteousness—God's nature was completely embodied in him. Nowhere was this more forcefully demonstrated than through his death on our behalf. By hating sin, God showed justice. By forgiving sin, he showed mercy. But by *being the payment* for that sin himself, he showed matchless, marvelous, magnificent grace.

What God Is

This, then, is what God is like. Theologians have come up with words that summarize these qualities, or "attributes," as they're known. Once we get past the somewhat formal feel of these terms, they can be useful tools to encapsulate what we know about God. Here's a list of his main attributes.

WAYS WE CAN'T BE LIKE GOD:

- *Omnipresent:* God is always near; no place is farther from him than any other place; he is not limited to any spatial dimensions.
- *Omnipotent:* God can do anything that doesn't violate his nature; he's all-powerful; nothing is impossible for him; his power is unlimited and unrestricted except by his own choice.
- *Omniscient:* God knows everything; nothing is hidden; nothing goes unnoticed; no situation is beyond his ability to grasp; all mysteries are clear to him; no one can tell him something he doesn't already know.
- *Sovereign:* God is the ultimate ruler of the universe; no one is greater in authority or power than he; no sin or disobedience can thwart the purposes he desires to bring to pass.
- *Eternal:* God has always been; he will always be; he had no beginning; he will have no end; he is the creator of time; he is not subject to time but rules over it.

- *Immutable*: God doesn't change; he isn't getting better; his beauty can't be diminished; he doesn't grow or increase; he's perfect the way he is; we can rest assured he will continue that way.
- *Infinite*: God is unlimited; whatever he is, he is to an infinite degree; we can't measure any part of him or his attributes; he is inexhaustible in every aspect of his being.

WAYS WE SHOULD IMITATE GOD:

- *Holy*: God is pure; he's without fault; he can't be compared to anyone or anything because he's so different from all we've known or experienced.
- *Wise*: God uses his knowledge skillfully; he makes sense; he is no fool; his counsel can be trusted.
- *Good*: God has no evil and can do no evil; he works for the benefit of his creatures; he can be trusted with our well-being.
- *Just*: God is fair; he doesn't tolerate unrighteousness; he will make sure every wrong will be made right; he is impartial.
- *Loving*: Sacrifice is in God's very nature; he cares; he gives; he serves; he works to bring about what we need; he's compassionate; he's sensitive; he chooses to let us matter to him.

We can come up with many other words that describe God as well: among them merciful, kind, pure, righteous, patient, faithful, trustworthy, generous, awesome, and majestic. These qualities will all be, to some degree, aspects of the main attributes we've listed above.

The more you get to know the Bible, the more you will discover the manifold descriptions of his nature. Look for new ways of describing him. Worship him for the many and varied facets of his being. Learn who he really is so you can gradually replace the shadows in your mind with the substance of his true nature.

What is God like? Maybe this classic children's song says it best: "Jesus loves me, this I know; for the Bible tells me so. . . ."

GOD'S WORD

PERSONAL STUDY: 1 John 3–5; James 1–2

SCRIPTURE MEMORY: 2 Timothy 3:16–17; Psalm 119:11

ON YOUR OWN: Scripture and the Benefits of a Relationship with God

"A thorough knowledge of the Bible is worth more than a college education."

—THEODORE ROOSEVELT

God's Word *to* You

Think back to a time when you received a card or email from a close friend or a special someone who was away on summer vacation or for the school year. How did you feel when you saw who it was from? How long did you wait to read the card or open the email?

When someone special leaves a message for you, you want to know the contents. It is puzzling to consider, then, that while many Christians are interested in knowing what God is saying to them, they neglect to read the letters and messages he has prepared for them. The Bible is God's love letter to all who trust in Christ. It only makes sense that they should want to learn all they can about God's Word, for it is his primary means of speaking to them.

This lesson will help you understand the value of personal Bible study (God's Word *to* you), show how Bible study allows you to uncover truths that can transform your character (God's Word *in* you), and reveal how you can take those truths to heart and carry them with you by memorizing Scripture (God's Word *with* you).

Five Ways to Grasp God's Word

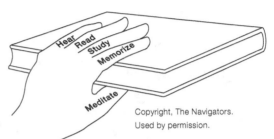

- Hear the Word (see Romans 10:17).
- Read the Word (see Revelation 1:3).
- Study the Word (see Acts 17:11).
- Memorize the Word (see Psalm 119:11).
- Meditate on the Word (see Psalm 1:2–3).

Copyright, The Navigators.
Used by permission.

1. Which of these ways of interacting with Scripture do you do most often? Which would you like to increase doing?

What God's Word Will Do for You

2. *It will help you grow spiritually* (see 1 Peter 2:2). What parallels can you see between an infant and its food and a Christian and the Bible?

3. *It will help you be honest with yourself* (see Hebrews 4:12). How does it feel to be penetrated by God's truth "even to dividing soul and spirit"?

4. *It will equip you for good work* (see 2 Timothy 3:16–17). In what ways does the Bible shape your character? How does it equip you to do what God wants you to do?

5. *It will renew your mind* (see Romans 12:2). In what ways can God's Word renew your mind?

6. *It will help you be successful in life* (see Joshua 1:8). What is your view of success?

7. *It will put truth at your fingertips* (see 2 Timothy 2:15). What are some specific parallels between a workman and his tools and the Christian and his or her Bible?

8. *It will protect you from attack* (see Ephesians 6:17). How does the way a soldier uses a sword compare with how a Christian can use the Word?

9. *It will influence others* (see Deuteronomy 6:6–7). How does the Bible help you to have a spiritual influence on your family and on others?

God's Word *in* You

The difference between reading the Bible and studying it is as simple as picking up a pen (or keypad) and *recording things*. When you ponder what you read and then write out your thoughts, you can achieve greater clarity and make lessons learned easier to integrate into your life. In the same way that you might find a rare nugget of gold lying on the ground, you can happen on some valuable truths by simply browsing through the pages of the Bible. But to find a richer vein of gold, you have to go beneath the surface—and this requires study.

Approaches to Personal Bible Study

10. *The sitters.* These people do not personally study the Bible but "sit at the feet" of those who explain Scripture to them. What are the sitters missing by not studying the Bible for themselves?

11. *The skimmers.* These people go beyond the sitters and actually read God's Word, and they may also regularly read some kind of daily devotional book. What do the skimmers miss by not going deeper into the Word?

12. *The scholars.* This group, though small in number, is most at home when studying the Bible in a scholarly manner, assisted by commentaries, Bible dictionaries, and other reference tools. Why might the scholars find that their methods do not necessarily produce spiritual growth?

13. *The students.* This is the best approach of all. According to Paul in 2 Timothy 2:15, what qualities does the "worker" or student of God's Word possess?

Three-Step Inductive Bible Study Method

14. *First, READ the Text ("What It Says").* Read the passage several times, preferably in a few different translations. Find out about the background and context of the book you're studying. How would you reply to someone who said you don't need to understand the context or background of a Bible passage because, they say, "It's God's timeless truth, all you have to do is read it and the Holy Spirit will teach you"?

15. *Second, MAKE Observations ("What It Teaches").* Why might it help your learning to restate (or rewrite) a passage in your own words and note a few simple observations about it?

16. *Third, APPLY What You Learn ("What to Do").* What is the difference between what a text *says* and what it *says to do?*

Practice the Method

Practice this method by turning to James 1:2–4 and completing the following:

17. What is the *background and context* for the passage?

18. What do you *observe* is being taught by the passage?

19. Which of the following can you *apply* from the passage?

☐ A promise to claim:

☐ A command to obey:

☐ A sin to confess:

☐ An example to follow:

☐ A behavior to change:

☐ An encouragement to receive:

☐ An insight to gain:

☐ An issue to pray about:

☐ A reason to worship God:

God's Word *with* You

Imagine you are a carpenter starting your day at a new work site. As you begin your first task, you remember that all your tools are at home in your basement! You drive back home, get your hammer, and return to work. The same thing happens when you need a saw. Everyone else on the job is frustrated by the slowdown of having to wait for you.

This pattern continues the rest of the day. Every time you need a tool, you have to go home and get it. The situation gets worse later when you cut your hand. The ambulance arrives within minutes, but the paramedics have to return to the hospital to get *their* equipment. They promise to get back to you as soon as they can.

This whole situation would be intolerable because of one obvious oversight: those who needed their tools didn't have them *when* and *where* those tools were needed. Yet many Christians approach their daily activities with a similar unpreparedness. They neglect to carry the truths and promises of God's Word with them.

As a Christian, you need more than just a familiarity with the Scriptures—you need knowledge of what God says *in the very moment of need*. One of the best ways to have God's Word readily accessible is through memorization. This study will help you understand the importance and benefits of memorizing Scripture.

Ten Great Reasons to Memorize Scripture

- It will purify your thoughts (see Philippians 4:8).
- It will increase your effectiveness in prayer (see John 15:7).
- It will help you in witnessing to others (see Acts 8:35–36).
- It will help you meditate on God's truth (see Psalm 119:97).

- It will enrich your Bible study (see 2 Timothy 3:16).
- It will enhance your counseling or teaching (see Proverbs 15:23).
- It will provide guidance for decisions (see Psalm 119:24).
- It will provide encouragement when you're feeling down (see Romans 15:4).
- It will strengthen you when you are tempted (see Psalm 37:31).
- It will increase your faith (see Romans 10:17).

20. Which of these reasons have you found valuable? Which would you like to have more of?

21. *Read Luke 4:1–13.* What do you observe about Jesus' responses to the Devil? In what situations might having passages of Scripture committed to memory be helpful?

Helps for Memorization

22. What do you see as the value of the following steps?

Focus on the benefit	
Know the meaning	
Use your imagination	
Don't forget to review	
Involve others	

Meditation and Memorization

23. What does it mean to meditate on God's Word? How does memorizing Scripture aid in doing that?

24. *Read Psalm 119:97.* When might be the best time of the day for you to focus intentionally on meditating on Scripture?

Your Walk with God

Bible

Schedule three times this week to be alone with God. Each day, read the passage indicated below and answer the questions that follow.

DAY ONE: 1 JOHN 3–5

Some truths in these chapters that have to do with loving others:

Some truths in these chapters that have to do with loving God:

Some truths in these chapters that have to do with receiving love from God:

DAY TWO: JAMES 1

Some of the things I observe in this passage:

One idea for how to apply this passage to my life:

DAY THREE: JAMES 2

Some of the things I observe in this passage:

One idea for how to apply this passage to my life:

Prayer

Pray for another person this week and for a particular ministry within your church. Also pray that God will help you memorize his Word and internalize it so that you are better able to do what the Bible says (see James 1:22). At the end of the week, list two or three benefits you received from these appointments with God.

Scripture Memory

Memorize these verses this week:

> *All Scripture is God-breathed and is useful for teaching, rebuking, correcting and training in righteousness, so that the servant of God may be thoroughly equipped for every good work* (2 Timothy 3:16–17).

> *I have hidden your word in my heart that I might not sin against you* (Psalm 119:11).

In the next study, we will begin to explore the topic of prayer. To prepare, think about a time when you prayed for something specific. What happened or didn't happen as a result of your prayer? What principles about prayer would you want to impress on a new believer?

On Your Own: Scripture and the Benefits of a Relationship with God

In the previous lesson, we learned that God is a friend worth having. In this lesson, we considered the important role Scripture plays in the daily life of a believer. The Bible is God's main vehicle for teaching us, but it is important to realize that he doesn't just want us to know lots of random facts. He instructs us so we can know him as he is and do his work in the world. As we get to know Scripture, we get to know God.

The Bible enables us to have a relationship with God, and, as a result, we receive many wonderful blessings. It's worth it for us to consider those blessings from time to time and reflect on the benefits we receive. Here are just a few:

- *Our relationships:* Our friendships, interactions with fellow workers, and even marriages can be renewed when we are in a right relationship with God. Scripture teaches us how to treat each other, and by following God's commandments, we experience a new level of love, concern, and relational depth for others. On top of that, as we gather in a local church with other believers to hear God's Word and study it together, we will inevitably meet new people—some like us and some different—who will enrich our lives (and we, in turn, will enrich their lives).

- *Our peace:* The restlessness we feel, produced by unforgiven sin and purposeless activities, ceases when we are in relationship with God. God's Word assures us we are now his children and guides us in the paths of righteousness. St. Augustine (AD 354–430) said, "You have made us for yourself, O God, and our hearts are restless until they find their rest in you." In God we have peace; his words lead us to restful green pastures.

- *Our purpose:* At best, a life without Christ will be given over to some lesser cause; at worst, it will degenerate into an existence of pleasure-seeking and selfishness. With Christ, our lives come under the direction and guidance of an all-loving Spirit who has our best interests continuously in mind. Through his Word, we are led to a life that has significance. Any and every action we do in the Spirit has eternal value. Every act of obedience brings a blessing in some fashion. This is not always seen in the present, but if nothing else, we know that God is pleased with us.

- *Our sense of fulfillment:* A deep, abiding satisfaction is the birthright of every believer, and as we mature, we experience it in increasing measure. Even hard times do not diminish our sense of joy because we know God is with us. His Word will not return void; it will continue changing and molding us, helping us to grow into the best version of ourselves—the man or woman whom God created us to be.

- *Our direction:* Through our relationship with God, we are given the counsel of an infinitely wise Adviser to assist our limited and finite human perspectives. The words that Jesus said to us—if we build on them—will enable us to survive any storm, and all decisions, big or small, become God's concerns as well as our own. The Scriptures provide a lamp for our feet and a light for our path (see Psalm 119:105). Although God also gives us common sense to help us make choices, when we acknowledge God in all our ways, it leads to a future that is bright. God invests himself for the good of all his children, and the outcome of every choice we make in obedience to his Word brings him glory and keeps us going in the right direction.

■ *Our confidence:* In 1 John 4:18 we read, "Perfect love drives out fear." God's Word teaches us how to overcome our fears, which includes fear of punishment (Christ already took that); fear of failure ("If God is for us, who can be against us?" Romans 8:31); fear of intimidation (none of our enemies are a match for the Lord); fear of loss (all that we have now belongs to Christ—his glory in us will never be hindered by any material or circumstantial fluctuations); fear of rejection (even if all others abandon us, he will never leave us nor forsake us; see Hebrews 13:5). When we believe what God says about us, all those fears give way to a settled confidence that all will be well.

■ *Our self-esteem:* We usually do not see ourselves for who we really are; we view ourselves as what we think others think we are. If parents and others have constantly found fault with us, we will find fault with ourselves. No matter how objective we try to be about it, our self-esteem is, to some extent, at the mercy of those we consider important to us. When God and his Word become important to us, his view of us will supersede all others—and Scripture abounds with promises that he loves us and that we are precious to him. We are engraved on the palms of his hands (see Isaiah 49:16)!

We receive all of these benefits and more . . . because we have a relationship with God grounded in his Word!

"Every problem a person has is related to his concept of God. If you have a big God, you have small problems. If you have a small God, you have big problems. It's as simple as that. When your God is big, then every seeming problem becomes an opportunity. When your God is small, every problem becomes an obstacle."

—WALTER A. HENRICHSEN, *DISCIPLES ARE MADE, NOT BORN*

GROUND RULES FOR PRAYER

PERSONAL STUDY: James 3:1–18
SCRIPTURE MEMORY: Philippians 4:6–7
ON YOUR OWN: Why Pray?

"In prayer it is better to have a heart without words than words without a heart."

—JOHN BUNYAN

The Power of Prayer

Would you prefer reading a book by candlelight or by a bright overhead light? If you are like most people, you would choose the overhead light. Although candlelight has a certain beauty about it, it's quite limited in the amount of light it can give. Besides, a gust of wind could blow it out or someone could easily extinguish it. To accomplish any amount of reading without severe eyestrain, you need the overhead light to illuminate the book's pages. And to get this light, you must use a switch.

In the spiritual realm, prayer is the switch that allows the power of the Holy Spirit to illuminate your life. Many Christians live their lives guided only by their own natural light, their own wisdom and power. But by using the switch of prayer, the Holy Spirit intercedes and causes the Father's light to bathe your life. Prayer is the difference—the power is there already. It just has to be "switched on." This study will help you understand how God answers prayer. You will explore four principles of prayer from the Bible and the four kinds of answers that God gives.

Principles of Prayer

1. *The Holy Spirit helps you know what and how to pray* (see Romans 8:26). In what ways are you weak when it comes to prayer?

2. When was a time you were frustrated with not knowing how to pray? Explain.

3. *The Holy Spirit intercedes on your behalf* (see Romans 8:26). What do you think are some of the benefits of having the Holy Spirit pray for you while you pray?

4. *God hears your heart in prayer more than your words* (see Romans 8:27). What is comforting about the promise that God searches and knows our hearts?

5. What cautions regarding prayer does Jesus mention in Matthew 6:5–8?

6. *Prayer is always answered* (see Romans 8:28–29). In what ways might God be at work even when he doesn't give an immediate "yes" to our prayers?

Four Ways God Answers Prayer

7. *No—your request is wrong* (see Matthew 26:36–39). What are some examples of prayer requests you know God would say "no" to?

8. *Slow—your timing is wrong* (see John 11:1–6). What are some examples of prayer requests that God might say "slow" to?

9. *Grow—your spiritual condition is wrong* (see James 4:2–3). In what ways might God ask you to grow before he gives you a "yes" to a prayer?

10. *Go—your request, timing, and spiritual condition are okay* (see Acts 12:5–17).
    What are some of your prayers that God has answered with a "yes"?

"Invariable 'success' in prayer would not prove the Christian doctrine at all. It would prove something much more like magic—a power in certain human beings to control, or compel, the course of nature. . . . A man who knew empirically that an event had been caused by his prayer would feel like a magician. His head would turn and his heart would be corrupted. The Christian is not to ask whether this or that event happened because of a prayer. He is rather to believe that all events without exception are answers to *prayer in the sense that whether they are grantings or refusals, the prayers of all concerned and their needs have all been taken into account. All prayers are heard, though not all prayers are granted."*

—C. S. LEWIS

Let's Pray

In this section, you will be given a simple method for a more balanced prayer life. The first part will present the ACTS outline to help you structure your prayers. This will allow you to overcome the natural tendency to pray only about things you want. The second part will allow you and your group members to practice the ACTS pattern for prayer.

ACTS: A Way to Pray

11. *Adoration* (see Psalm 100:1–5). How do you express adoration to God?

12. What benefits come to you from praising God?

13. *Confession* (see 1 John 1:9). Why is it difficult to confess your sin to God?

14. What does God promise he will do when you confess your sin?

15. *Thanksgiving* (see Luke 17:11–19). What excuses keep you from giving thanks to God?

16. *Supplication* (see Philippians 4:6–7). What are some specific examples of requests you can bring to God in prayer?

17. What role does faith play in supplication?

Prayer Time

As a group, end the meeting with an extended time of prayer together. First, take a few moments to fill in the blanks below with some ideas for praying. Then, after everyone has had a chance to do this, go around the circle and ask all in the group who are comfortable doing so to pray. The group leader will close.

18. *Adoration:* "Father, I want to praise you for being . . ."

19. *Confession:* "Here are some sinful behaviors, thoughts, or attitudes I would like to confess . . ."

20. *Thanksgiving:* "Thank you, Lord, for all my blessings and for giving me . . ."

21. *Supplication:* "I would like to bring these concerns that are on my mind today and have everyone here agree in prayer for them . . ."

Apply It to Your Life

22. Now that the group prayer time is over, what will it take for you to become a person who prays more?

Your Walk with God

Bible

Schedule three times this week to be alone with God. Each day, read the passage indicated below and answer the questions that follow. Also, reread the Scripture passages from the "Four Ways God Answers Prayer" section in this lesson.

DAY ONE: JAMES 3:1–5

Some of the things I observe in this passage:

One idea for how to apply this passage to my life:

DAY TWO: JAMES 3:6–12

Some of the things I observe in this passage:

One idea for how to apply this passage to my life:

DAY THREE: JAMES 3:13–18

Some of the things I observe in this passage:

One idea for how to apply this passage to my life:

Prayer

Spend a few minutes praying about those areas in life where you need God's wisdom and strength. At the end of the week, list two or three benefits you received from these appointments with God.

Scripture Memory

Memorize these verses this week:

> *Do not be anxious about anything, but in every situation, by prayer and petition, with thanksgiving, present your requests to God. And the peace of God, which transcends all understanding, will guard your hearts and your minds in Christ Jesus* (Philippians 4:6–7).

In the next study, we will examine how regular quiet times can enhance our walk with God. To prepare for the session, think about what you like most and least about your current prayer life. What is one area of your walk with God in which you could use some help?

On Your Own: Why Pray?

When people think about praying, the question often asked is, "Why bother to pray at all?" God knows everything, so what's the point of pretending to "inform" him with our words? Furthermore, what makes us think our requests have any bearing on what God is going to do? Since God is in charge and certainly knows what's best, why would we think our wishes have any effect on his choices? If what we want *isn't* right for all concerned, he shouldn't do it regardless of our requests. And if what we want *is* the best for all (and not just for us), being a good God, he would have chosen that regardless of our asking for it.

Tough questions! And yet Jesus encouraged us to pray, so there must be good reasons for us to engage in it.

The first thing to realize is that we don't have to understand how prayer works for us to choose to do it and discover it is worthwhile. Many things are of value and yet are a mystery to us. Take technology, for example. Most people use a smartphone, but few really understand how it works. Most just know that when they turn on the phone, they can make calls or text or do many other things without having a clue of how it all happens. Likewise, prayer is valuable to us even if we don't get all the theology or mechanics of it. People who pray will tell you that when they pray, life just seems to go better, and they get better. Even if all their requests are not met with a "yes" from God, they sense praying was still beneficial.

This leads to the second consideration: if prayer is just trying to get something from God—wanting something to happen that otherwise wouldn't happen—then we are bound to be disappointed from time to time. But the Bible records many prayers that have nothing to do with people wanting God to do anything other than listen to them and connect with them.

Think of it this way: if the only time your spouse came to you was with a request for you to do something, you wouldn't be too happy with the relationship.

On the other hand, if you and your spouse enjoy talking, like sharing experiences, express love and affection in a variety of ways, *and then* from time to time make requests of each other, that's a much better relationship. Prayer is certainly not just asking for things. Prayer has value because it builds our relationship with God regardless of any requests we may or may not make of him.

We must also note that Jesus taught that God *does indeed* partner with us through prayer—he does seem to do some things at our request and not do other things if we don't ask. It's as if God has a long list of things he's going to do whether or not anybody asks, but then he has another list of "options"—things he has sovereignly chosen to do (or not do) depending on what we request in prayer. He is willing; but he is also waiting. As James wrote, "You do not have because you do not ask God" (James 4:2).

By way of analogy, if we don't eat, we will be hungry. After we eat, the hunger goes away. What we do or don't do affects how we feel and how healthy we are. God doesn't "determine" if we eat or not—that's our choice. But if we eat, he's set it up so our bodies will get what they need. The same is true with prayer. If we pray, some things will happen—or not happen—because of that choice. God set it up that way. The reasons for that may be a mystery, but to be alive and have free will means, at the very least, that our choices have consequences. Our choices to pray or not pray—like our choices to love or not love, harm or not harm, care or not care, eat or not eat—have real consequences in the world.

C. S. Lewis wrote about how prayer and the will of God work this way: "Infinite wisdom does not need telling what is best, and infinite goodness needs no urging to do it. But neither does God need any of those things that are done by finite agents, whether living or inanimate. He could, if He chose, repair our bodies miraculously without food; or give us food without the aid of farmers, bakers and butchers; or knowledge without the aid of learned men; or convert the heathen without missionaries. Instead, He allows soils and weather and animals and the muscles, minds and wills of men to cooperate in the execution of His Will. 'God,' said Pascal, 'instituted prayer in order to lend to His creatures the dignity of causality.'"

Finally, we who follow Jesus see his example of praying and know it is a good idea. We may not know why. But we see that Jesus prayed often, prayed with passion, and talked to his Father both casually and formally, and because of that, we should do likewise. We certainly know Jesus didn't think his prayers were informing his Father of anything. But just as a parent delights in a child telling a story even if he or she has heard it before, God takes delight in our sharing our thoughts and feelings with him, even though he knows every detail before we speak it.

If all else fails, try this experiment. For two weeks, simply increase how often you pray, vary the way you pray, and enlarge the scope of what you pray for. Then notice how you feel and what has happened during those two weeks. Even if you don't see much different happening "out there," notice the condition of your heart. Are you closer to God? Do you have a greater sense of his presence? Are you more in tune with him and living more like how you've always wanted to live?

The great thing about prayer is that simply doing it provides the confirmation that it is a good thing to do!

GETTING TOGETHER WITH GOD

PERSONAL STUDY: James 4–5
SCRIPTURE MEMORY: 1 Thessalonians 5:16–18
ON YOUR OWN: Jesus' Quiet Times

"Prayer is not learned in a classroom but in the closet."

—E. M. Bounds

Time to Be with God

After driving through miles of gridlock to arrive early to work, a busy executive closes his office door to enjoy a few moments of quiet before the phones begin ringing . . . a frazzled mother puts her noisy children to bed and plops down on the couch in the stillness of the evening to talk at last with her husband . . . a weary student takes a break from a frantic exam schedule to take an unhurried walk around campus.

What do all these people have in common? They need times of quiet and calm to relax, think about the day, and build relationships with friends and family. In a similar way, you also need times of quiet and prayerful reflection with Jesus and his Word to build your relationship with him. How do you do that? Scheduling regular quiet times is a good way to start. This study will give you some practical advice for how to establish regular times for personal devotions.

What Is a Quiet Time?

1. How would you describe a good quiet time?

2. What do you do during your times alone with God?

Making the Time

3. Why is it sometimes difficult for you to find time for personal devotions?

4. What are some common distractions that get in the way of your quiet time with God?

5. Here are some ways to find time in a crowded schedule:

■ Listen to a recording of worshipful music as you drive, work around the house, or get ready for the day.

■ Walk or ride to a forest preserve, the country, or other place of natural beauty.

■ Sing worshipful songs to the Lord.

■ Occasionally vary your quiet time routine so that you don't get stuck in a rut.

Which of these ideas appeal the most to you? Why?

6. What could you do to make your times alone with God more meaningful?

"The reason God seeks our praise is not because
he won't be fully God until he gets it, but
that we won't be happy until we give it."

—JOHN PIPER

Studying the Bible

7. What are some ways that you currently study the Bible? How effective are those methods in terms of remembering what you've read?

8. What hinders you from getting more out of personal Bible study?

9. Here are some ways to vary your study of the Scripture:

- Use a concordance or online tools to study a specific topic, character trait, or Bible character.
- Use the cross-references in your Bible to compare other places in Scripture where the same word is used or idea is taught.
- Meditate on a passage by creating vivid mental pictures of the story or event.
- Rewrite the passage, using contemporary wording or your own circumstances as the setting.
- Mark interesting phrases that stand out to you.
- Write down questions as you read.
- Write a short title to describe the passage you are reading.
- Listen to a recording of the Bible being read or dramatically reenacted.

   Which of these ideas appeal the most to you? Why?

10. What are some other creative ways of making your Bible study more meaningful?

Praying

11. How would you describe the way you communicate with God in your life? In which places and situations do you tend to pray the most?

12. What prevents you from praying consistently?

13. Here are some other variations you can use to keep your prayer life fresh:
    - Write out your prayers.
    - Keep a prayer journal to record your prayers and answers.
    - Vary the ACTS pattern so that you spend one day in adoration, another in confession, and so on.
    - Put away your prayer list and simply talk to God.
    - Go on a prayer walk—for a specific reason or just to pray in a mindful, active way.
    - Vary your position, posture, or location when you pray.

    Which of these ideas appeal the most to you? Why?

14. What other ideas do you have to make your prayer time more effective?

Action Plan

15. What is the best time of day and location for you to have your quiet time?

16. What are the most likely distractions or interruptions you will face?

17. What can you do to prevent these distractions or interruptions?

18. What steps will you take today to make sure you have a consistent quiet time with God?

Your Walk with God

Bible

Schedule three times this week to be alone with God. Each day, read the passage indicated below and answer the questions that follow.

DAY ONE: JAMES 4:1–10

Some of the things I observe in this passage:

One idea for how to apply this passage to my life:

DAY TWO: JAMES 4:11–5:6

Some of the things I observe in this passage:

One idea for how to apply this passage to my life:

DAY THREE: JAMES 5:7–20

Some of the things I observe in this passage:

One idea for how to apply this passage to my life:

Prayer

Spend a few minutes asking God to make you become the kind of person who does what the Bible says (see James 1:2). Also practice each of the four aspects of prayer—one each day:

Day One: Praise God using Psalm 23.

Day Two: Identify the main areas of temptation you struggle with. Confess any sin in these areas and pray for strength.

Day Three: Recall several spiritual, physical, and relational blessings. Thank God for each one.

Day Four: Pray for any major concerns in your life and in the lives of others who are close to you.

At the end of the week, list two or three benefits you received from these appointments with God.

Scripture Memory

Memorize these verses this week:

> *Rejoice always, pray continually, give thanks in all circumstances; for this is God's will for you in Christ Jesus* (1 Thessalonians 5:16–18).

Next time, we will begin the first of two studies on the Holy Spirit. To prepare, recall how you first learned about the Holy Spirit.

On Your Own: Jesus' Quiet Times

Theologically, Jesus and the Father were one (see John 10:30). This has been true from eternity and is still true today. They can never be more "one" than they are now or always have been. Yet to stay in vital connection, when Jesus was here on earth, he set aside time to be alone with his Father. Like two people with a good marriage, he and God the Father enjoyed each other's company and spent time with one another when nothing else was going on except for them being together.

It can be instructive to look at some of those times when Jesus was alone with the Father, ponder why that was, and examine what can be learned from Jesus' example. During the next several days, reflect on the following examples of Jesus' "quiet times." What are some of the ways you can do as he did, so your life also reflects the presence and power of God?

Forty Days in the Wilderness (Matthew 4:1–11)

Right after Jesus was baptized and before he started his public ministry, he spent more than a month alone with God at the leading of the Spirit. What is significant about this time of solitude was that Jesus was also in the presence of the Devil! This was not just a time for him to be away from the life he had known up until then; it was a key time to prepare him for ministry.

The temptations the Devil threw at Jesus were the same temptations that would come up again and again during his ministry. They culminated when he had to go to the cross at the end of his life—where he faced these exact temptations one final time in the most intense way. By dealing with them first in the wilderness, he prepared himself for when they would come to him later. From this, we can observe that time alone with God may also be a place of preparation for resisting temptation and a way to strengthen our resolve to be obedient.

Choosing the Twelve Apostles (Mark 3:13–19; Luke 6:12–16)

One of the most significant aspects of Jesus' ministry strategy was to train a select group of people who would carry on his work after he left. The ones he chose to invest in would determine the success of his plan over the long haul. So, to make that decision, he first gathered some men around him and watched them while they participated in his work alongside him. Jesus got to see them in action, which was an important first step in the vetting process.

But it was not enough for Jesus to simply look at their mere outward and human qualities. He needed to know who his Father wanted him to choose for this special assignment. So Jesus spent the night in prayer, and only after getting affirmation from the Father was he ready to make his choice of the Twelve.

Pursuing a New Direction in Ministry (Luke 4:42–43)

Jesus went to be alone with the Father when he was in the midst of a productive ministry season. The people were delighted in what Jesus was doing, and no one could deny that he was having a powerful impact in that region. And yet it appears that while he was alone with God, he realized that he had to move on to visit other towns.

The people did not want him to do this. It was only by spending time alone with the Father that Jesus could think through his ministry strategy and then decide to do something the people might interpret as "uncaring." It was only through his time alone with God that he could choose to leave them—what they might consider "abandoning" them—right when there were so many powerful things happening.

In our lives, tough ministry decisions may have to be made. Time alone with God may be the only place where we can hear new marching orders from him. There, we can fortify ourselves to do what he's calling us to do, even when it might not be popular.

Replenishment from Busyness (Mark 6:30–31; 7:24; 9:2)

Like any good leader, Jesus had seasons of intense busyness. But also like a good leader, he knew his human limitations required him to periodically set aside time to pull away from the crowds and do something that would replenish him. Part of what provided that restoration and renewal was spending time in solitude and prayer. Jesus got to a point where he had to set aside the work of God *through* him so that he could cultivate the work of God *in* him. With that renewed energy and refocus, he could return to the demands of his ministry and face whatever he needed to face.

Preparation for the Cross (Matthew 26:36–46; Mark 14:32–42; Luke 22:39–46)

The most significant event in all of Jesus' life was his death on the cross. In order to be ready to face the excruciating pain and hardship that would require, he needed some time alone with his disciples and his heavenly Father. So Jesus first had a Passover meal with his disciples, and then he took them with him to a quiet place to pray.

Jesus chose three of his twelve followers—Peter, James, and John—to go with him to an "inner sanctuary" of prayer, where he asked them to support him. He then went a bit farther to spend time by himself, praying and getting strength from his Father. The anguish of that time was evident by the description of his physical symptoms we find in the Gospels: drops of sweat covering him like (or could they have actually been?) drops of blood.

Although Jesus was God in the flesh, he was also a human being and had limitations associated with being human. He knew he was soon going to be betrayed, denied, and deserted by those he loved the most. He knew that the flogging, followed by being nailed to a cross, was going to be unimaginably painful. He knew he would feel the weight of the world's sin on him. So he chose to do the most empowering, sustaining thing he could think of doing: spend some time with God the Father in prayer.

THE ROLE OF THE HOLY SPIRIT

PERSONAL STUDY: Philippians 1–2
SCRIPTURE MEMORY: Ephesians 5:18; Galatians 2:20
ON YOUR OWN: More on the Role of the Holy Spirit

"If we think of the Holy Spirit . . . as merely a power or influence, our constant thought will be, 'How can I get more of the Holy Spirit,' but if we think of Him in the Biblical way as a Divine Person, our thought will rather be, 'How can the Holy Spirit have more of me?'"

—R. A. TORREY

Who Is the Holy Spirit?

Think for a moment about the way wind affects your life. It can be a gentle waft that refreshes you on a hot day. It might be the steady breeze that keeps a child's kite aloft and guides a sailboat to its destination. Then too the wind can be a tremendous force of nature, whipping snow into gigantic snowdrifts, knocking down power lines, and grounding airplanes. It can even be a tornado or cyclone, leaving destruction in its path. Each of us must learn to respect its power, or we may find ourselves in danger.

Jesus compared the Holy Spirit to wind (see John 3:8). Like the wind, the Spirit can assist you in your efforts to please God, and he can also intervene to discourage you from sinful activity. His power must not be resisted, however, because to do so affronts God and will cut you off from your Source. Cooperation with the Holy Spirit is essential for any Christian's walk with God. But who is the Holy Spirit, and what does he do? This study will help you understand the person and work of the Holy Spirit.

1. What titles does Jesus use in John 14:16–17 to describe the Holy Spirit?

2. According to Jesus, who sent the Holy Spirit (see John 14:26)?

3. Why can't the world accept the Spirit (see John 14:17)?

4. In what way does the Holy Spirit convict us (see John 16:7–11)?

5. How does the Holy Spirit guide and teach us (see John 14:26; 16:12–15)?

6. How does the Holy Spirit help to save us (see Titus 3:5)?

7. What does it mean when we say the Holy Spirit reassures us (see Romans 8:15–16)?

8. In what way is the Spirit like a deposit (see Ephesians 1:13–14)?

9. For what does the Holy Spirit empower us (see Acts 1:8)?

10. How does the Holy Spirit help us when we pray (see Romans 8:26)?

Being Filled with the Holy Spirit

Imagine filling two glasses with equal amounts of water. Into one glass you drop a seltzer tablet that is wrapped in a plastic bag. You notice that nothing happens—the plastic has prevented the tablet from dissolving in the water, and it just sits there. Next, you drop an unwrapped tablet into the other glass. The tablet fizzes exuberantly and fills the glass with thousands of small bubbles that are spread throughout.

This simple experiment illustrates how we should allow the Holy Spirit to work in our lives. Both glasses have the whole tablet—there's no more of the tablet to give. The difference is that in one glass the tablet is free to dissolve and affect every drop of water; in the other glass, conditions exist that inhibit the effectiveness of the tablet. A bigger tablet won't help; the plastic has to be removed.

When we do not face our sin, our disobedience acts like the plastic bag around the seltzer and robs us of the Spirit's dynamic influence. But when we are receptive and obedient to God, the Holy Spirit releases his energy into every part of our lives.

The Holy Spirit's Work

11. What is the Holy Spirit's role in the process of your spiritual growth (see Philippians 1:6)?

12. What is your role in the process of spiritual growth (see Ephesians 5:18)?

13. What does it mean to say that Christians should be "filled" with the Holy Spirit?

14. What are some things that being filled with the Spirit helps you to do (see Ephesians 5:19–21)?

15. How does being filled with the Spirit influence your character (see Galatians 5:22–23)?

Apply It to Your Life

16. In the illustration for this section, what does the plastic bag around the seltzer tablet represent? What would cause you to seal in or limit the power of the Spirit in your life?

17. How do you "unwrap" and turn loose the Holy Spirit in you?

18. What role of the Spirit impressed you in this study?

19. How would you summarize the ministry of the Holy Spirit to a new Christian?

20. In what areas of your life do you need the Holy Spirit to have greater influence?

Your Walk with God

Bible

Schedule three times this week to be alone with God. Each day, read the passage indicated below and answer the questions that follow.

DAY ONE: PHILIPPIANS 1:1–18

Some of the things I observe in this passage:

One idea for how to apply this passage to my life:

DAY TWO: PHILIPPIANS 1:19–2:11

Some of the things I observe in this passage:

One idea for how to apply this passage to my life:

DAY THREE: PHILIPPIANS 2:12–30

Some of the things I observe in this passage:

One idea for how to apply this passage to my life:

Prayer

On each of your three days with God this week, pray for the following:

Day One (Adoration): Meditate on Psalm 103:1–5 and express a prayer of adoration in your own words.

Day Two (Thanksgiving): Thank God for relationships with specific people who have been a blessing to you and others.

Day Three (Concerns): Pray for three of your own concerns and three from other people (you may pray about the concerns shared at the beginning of this study).

List some temptations you face and write down what you could do to better resist them.

Scripture Memory

Memorize these verses this week:

Do not get drunk on wine, which leads to debauchery. Instead, be filled with the Spirit (Ephesians 5:18).

I have been crucified with Christ and I no longer live, but Christ lives in me. The life I now live in the body, I live by faith in the Son of God, who loved me and gave himself for me (Galatians 2:20).

In the next study, we will look at how believers can be filled with the Spirit. We will also discuss how we can grieve the Holy Spirit—ways in which we hinder his work. To prepare, consider a habit that you had to learn over time. How did that behavior, practice, or discipline become second nature to you? Also think about the different ways a person can suppress or extinguish a fire. What parallels can you draw between those conditions and the ways a believer can put out the fire of the Holy Spirit?

On Your Own: More on the Role of the Holy Spirit

Imagine Jesus spending three years with you, inspiring you about all the new things the kingdom of God will bring on earth. Then imagine him saying, "Oh, by the way, I'm leaving you before any of that happens!" What a confusing message! And what heartbreak—to be abandoned by the leader you've come to love and want to follow for the rest of your life.

So when Jesus introduced the idea to his disciples that Someone—the Holy Spirit—would come to take his place and that they would not be alone, it was both comforting and baffling. Jesus went so far as to say it was actually advantageous for him to go away so the Holy Spirit could come (see John 16:7). The disciples surely wondered, *Who is the Holy Spirit? What is he going to do? How could he possibly make up for not having Jesus physically present?*

The Bible explains in a variety of places what the Holy Spirit does for us as believers. Those functions include the following:

- Advocating or interceding on our behalf
- Guiding our thoughts and actions
- Convicting us of sin
- Gifting us
- Empowering us
- Reminding us of who we are in Christ

Translators have used various English words to try to translate the title Jesus gave to the Spirit, including *advocate, counselor, friend, comforter,* and *helper.* In Greek, the word is *parakletos. Para* (our words *parallel* and *paralegal* have the same prefix) means "to be alongside." *Kletos* comes from the verb meaning "to call." So the Holy Spirit is the one "called to come alongside" us, advocating for us, counseling us, and helping us. The word also has legal connotations, evoking the idea of the Spirit acting as our counsel for defense in a court of law, advocating for us before a judge and pleading on our behalf.

The Holy Spirit Gives Us Power

Because of the Spirit within us, we have power to understand things we otherwise wouldn't, do things we might not otherwise be capable of doing, love those who are difficult to love, and have joy when we face difficulty. The apostle Paul wrote the following to one young church to remind them of the power they received from the Holy Spirit's presence in their lives:

> *For we know, brothers and sisters loved by God, that he has chosen you, because our gospel came to you not simply with words but also with power, with the Holy Spirit and deep conviction. You know how we lived among you for your sake. You became imitators of us and of the Lord, for you welcomed the message in the midst of severe suffering with the joy given by the Holy Spirit* (1 Thessalonians 1:4–6, emphasis added).

This short passage is packed with information about the Holy Spirit. We discover that the Holy Spirit gives us understanding that goes beyond words and beyond even intellectual understanding. The Holy Spirit convicts us, influencing both our attitudes and actions. We become empowered to be "imitators" of our godly mentors and of Jesus. Paul reminds us that the Holy Spirit also gives us joy in the midst of suffering.

The Holy Spirit Tells Us the Truth

The Spirit enables us to discern what is true—even those difficult truths about ourselves that we'd rather not face. The Spirit gives us supernatural insight, helping us to understand what would otherwise be beyond our grasp.

The Bible tells us that if we ask God for wisdom, we'll receive it (see James 1:5). And it is through the Holy Spirit that we receive that wisdom. When we read the words of the Bible, the Holy Spirit enables us to understand them at a deeper level; to attain not just intellectual understanding but also insight and a readiness to respond. When the words "leap off the page" and seem to specifically apply to us and our situation, that's the work of the Holy Spirit. And when we find ourselves recognizing that obedience will be hard, the Spirit encourages us to go in his power and do what is right (or stop doing what is wrong).

The Spirit keeps working even after we close our Bible. When we are faithful to read and study God's Word (or even memorize it), the Spirit will bring truth to our minds in specific situations where it is appropriate. As we go through our day, we can ask God to help and guide us; and through the Spirit, we'll receive power and insight and wisdom to make good decisions.

Beyond helping us to recall truth we've read in our Bibles, the Spirit can also speak to us by giving us thoughts or insights we'd likely not have on our own. In a conversation, the Spirit might give us words that we know we would never have come up with on our own (or help us know when to wisely shut our mouth!).

Sometimes, people wonder when they have a specific thought whether it's the Holy Spirit, just their own wishful thinking, or something else. Quite often, what the Spirit tells us will sound much like what is our deepest heart's desire because he is in us shaping our very wants to conform to God's (see Psalm 37:4; Philippians 2:13). That said, we must remember that God never contradicts himself, so the Spirit won't nudge us to do something contrary to the teachings of Jesus or the Bible.

The Holy Spirit Reminds Us

On our own, we tend to forget to walk in God's way. We easily revert to making decisions based on selfish motives or on our whims. This often gets us into trouble. Jesus said, "But the Advocate, the Holy Spirit, whom the Father will send in my name, will teach you all things and will remind you of everything I have said to you" (John 14:26). So another role of the Spirit is to remind us—to bring to consciousness (however often we need it)—God's truth and wisdom. And after the Spirit reminds us of the truth, he also enables us, supernaturally, to live according to that truth.

The Holy Spirit Convicts Us without Shame

The Holy Spirit also convicts us; that is, he lets us know when we've made choices that are wrong. By pointing out our sin, the Spirit helps us in the process of spiritual transformation. Conviction invites us to change.

In Romans 12:2, Paul says we're transformed by the renewing of our minds. This "re-minding" is, in fact, "remaking our mind"—a rewiring of our very brain synapses so that we literally think differently than we used to without his influence. The Spirit is actively participating in our transformation, steering us away from sin and toward Christlikeness.

However, the Holy Spirit convicts us lovingly and doesn't shame us. Shame says, *You're worthless, you're bad, you'll never change.* The Holy Spirit says, *You're valued, and I will help you to courageously make better choices.* He says, *You're loved, and God's way leads to life—let me help you walk in it.*

SPIRIT-DIRECTED LIVING

PERSONAL STUDY: Philippians 3–4
SCRIPTURE MEMORY: James 4:1
ON YOUR OWN: More on Spirit-Directed Living

"The way to be filled—controlled and dominated—by the Spirit is to place Christ at the center of our lives, instead of self. This only happens as we submit to Him—as we allow Him to become Lord of our lives."

—BILLY GRAHAM

How to Be Filled with the Holy Spirit

A brash young entrepreneur decides to start a business in a lucrative, high-tech field. Because he needs the help, he brings on board a top-flight consultant to function as his daily adviser. But instead of trusting in the consultant's wisdom, the entrepreneur decides to do things his way. He ignores directives about financial planning. He makes ill-advised decisions without his adviser's knowledge. He even keeps him out of important meetings. Predictably, the business fails within a short time.

Many Christians fail to realize their relationship with the Lord shares many of the same problems. These people know about the wisdom of a daily quiet time and may even want the Spirit to direct their lives. But they insist on doing things their own way. It comes as no surprise that they stumble again and again. These setbacks are entirely preventable, however. This study will show you how you can live in the Spirit more fully each day.

Surrender to Christ

1. What are Christians to put to death (see Colossians 3:1–5)?

2. What does it mean for a Christian to become a living sacrifice (see Romans 12:1–2)?

3. *Read Luke 18:22–23 and 19:5–8.* How would you compare the ways in which these two men faced the need to surrender to God?

SELF-DIRECTED LIVING

DRIVER SEAT   PASSENGER SEAT

4. What problems will result from a self-directed life?

SPIRIT-DIRECTED LIVING

DRIVER SEAT   PASSENGER SEAT

5. What traits will a Spirit-directed life produce?

Obey Christ

6. Once you have surrendered (an inward change), the next step is to obey (an outward change). What happens when Christians surrender but do not obey (see 1 John 2:3–6)?

7. List a few areas of your life that are important to you. What does it mean to obey Christ in each area?

Abide in Christ

8. To *abide* in Christ means to continue or remain in him. Why is abiding in Christ important (see John 15:1–11)?

9. How can you tell when you are not abiding in Christ?

Grieving the Holy Spirit

Imagine that you are sitting around a campfire on a cool autumn evening. The warmth of the flames makes you feel comfortable and content. You become lost in your thoughts when, without warning, a sudden shower pours down on your campsite. The leaping flames soon turn into flickers and then become smoldering ashes. Now you are wet and miserable, and the chill of the evening makes you long for the glow that you felt a few moments earlier.

In much the same way, you can quench the fire of the Holy Spirit with careless actions and sinful attitudes. Not only do you displease God, but you also become miserable. This study will help you understand what it means to grieve the Holy Spirit and how to get back in step with the Spirit when you do.

What It Means

10. What are some ways to cause a friend or parent grief? By analogy, what does it mean to grieve the Holy Spirit (see Ephesians 4:29–31)?

11. What does it mean to put out the Spirit's fire (see 1 Thessalonians 5:19–22)?

Ways to Grieve the Holy Spirit

12. *Active disobedience* (sins of commission). What are some examples of active disobedience (see Galatians 5:16–21)? Why does this grieve the Spirit?

13. *Passive disobedience* (sins of omission). What are some personal examples of knowing the right thing to do but not doing it (see James 4:17)?

14. *Being ashamed of Christ.* What consequences will a believer suffer for being ashamed of Christ (see Mark 8:38)? In what situations do you find it difficult to stand up for Christ?

15. *Lack of faith in Christ.* Read Mark 9:17–23. Who lacked faith in this story? Why does lack of faith grieve the Holy Spirit (see Hebrews 11:6)?

Apply It to Your Life

16. In what ways are you prone to grieve the Holy Spirit?

17. What should you do when you think you are grieving the Holy Spirit?

18. What is one step you can take to live in the Spirit more fully each day?

"It is the work of the Holy Spirit to make God something vastly more than a theological notion, no matter how orthodox; He is the Spirit of the living God, and it is His work to make God a living God to us, a Being whom we know, with whom we have personal acquaintance, a Being more real to us than the most intimate human friend we have."

—R. A. TORREY

Your Walk with God

Bible

Schedule three times this week to be alone with God. Each day, read the passage indicated below and answer the questions that follow.

DAY ONE: PHILIPPIANS 3:1–16

Some of the things I observe in this passage:

One idea for how to apply this passage to my life:

DAY TWO: PHILIPPIANS 3:17–4:9

Some of the things I observe in this passage:

One idea for how to apply this passage to my life:

DAY THREE: PHILIPPIANS 4:10–23

Some of the things I observe in this passage:

One idea for how to apply this passage to my life:

Prayer

Look up the following passages that relate to obeying Christ. On each of four days, pray for the two areas listed that should be surrendered to Christ's control.

Day One: The future (Proverbs 3:5–6; James 4:13–17) and relationships (Matthew 5:21–26; Romans 12:9–21). Also pray for members of your family who have emotional, physical, or relational needs.

Day Two: Work (Psalm 127:1–2; Colossians 3:22–4:1) and leisure (Mark 6:31–32; Ephesians 5:15–16). Praise God for his love and righteousness.

Day Three: Marriage (Matthew 19:4–6; 1 Peter 3:1–9) and children (Psalm 127:3–5; Colossians 3:21). (If you are single, choose another significant relationship.)

Day Four: Money (Psalm 112:5; 1 Corinthians 16:1–2) and possessions (Matthew 6:31–33; Luke 12:13–21). Pray about anything mentioned in this study if you sense the conviction of the Holy Spirit.

Scripture Memory

Memorize this verse this week:

Think about letting the Holy Spirit flow through you to others so you become a conduit of his grace.

Review Your Day

As your day comes to a close, take a few minutes to review all that happened. Where did you notice God? In what ways did you cooperate with the Holy Spirit and allow the fruit of the Spirit (love, joy, peace, patience, kindness, etc.) to flourish? In what ways did you notice you were walking through your day in step with the Spirit (see Galatians 5:16, 22–25)? What happened when you forgot about living a Spirit-directed life? Did you hear any whispers or promptings from the Spirit? Did you act on them or ignore them?

Have a conversation with God about the moments of your day. Ask the Holy Spirit to point out both the times you cooperated and the times you went your own way. Keep in mind his grace, which covers all your sins and faults. Rejoice and thank God for any progress you have made, and ask for help to do better tomorrow in those areas that were a struggle.

DEVELOPING INTIMACY WITH GOD

This review culminates your study of Part 1: "Developing Intimacy with God." Use this time to reflect on your small-group experience so far. This is also a time to appreciate and be grateful for what God has accomplished in you. This study will help you assess what you've learned and how you've grown.

Reflect on What You've Learned

1. Since we began, what have you found to be the most positive aspect of these studies?

2. What is a fresh insight or an old truth that has come alive through this study?

3. What area of your personal spiritual growth needs improvement?

4. How has your understanding of the Bible changed since you began this study?

5. What is one change you've noticed in your prayer life as a result of this study?

6. How would you describe the importance of quiet time to someone who just became a Christian?

7. What is the significance of the Holy Spirit in the life of the believer?

8. Currently, what is the greatest obstacle to your walk with God?

9. Ten years from now, what you like your walk with God to be like?

10. What are some things you would like everyone to pray for?

Self-Evaluation

Your group leader will be meeting with you to discuss your current spiritual condition and your hopes for growing in your faith. Please take some time to reflect honestly on where you stand right now within these four basic categories of Christian growth. Rate yourself in each category.

+   DOING WELL. I'M PLEASED WITH MY PROGRESS SO FAR.

X   ON THE RIGHT TRACK, BUT I SEE DEFINITE AREAS FOR IMPROVEMENT.

−   THIS IS A STRUGGLE. I NEED SOME HELP.

A Disciple Is One Who . . .

11. *Walks with God.* To what extent is my Bible study and prayer time adequate for helping me walk with God?

Rating: _____

Comments:

12. *Lives the Word.* To what extent is my mind filled with scriptural truths so that my actions and reactions show I am being transformed?

Rating: _____

Comments:

13. *Contributes to the work.* To what extent am I actively participating in the church with my time, talents, and treasures?

Rating: _____

Comments:

14. *Impacts the world.* To what extent am I impacting my world with a Christian witness and influence?

Rating: _____

Comments:

15. Other issues I would like to discuss with my small-group leader:

PART 2

GETTING TO KNOW JESUS

What do you do well? Most of us have some skill or distinguishing trait for which we're recognized. One person can work with cars; another person is knowledgeable about some branch of learning; and someone else has a great sense of humor. Some people are known for what they make, some for how they serve, some for what they do, others for what they say.

We're able to become proficient at our area of expertise through focus and practice. Then, whatever captivates our minds and hearts—whatever becomes second nature to us—impacts the world around us. It forms our identity. We become someone special to others by having something special to offer—and that flows from being attracted to and spending time absorbed in a special area of interest.

So, what does all this have to do with the importance of knowing Jesus?

The shared goal for us as believers, no matter how we're wired individually, is to become like Jesus. We don't all need to be experts at the same thing, but there is one thing at which we *all* must excel: *knowing Jesus.* If we call ourselves "Christians," we must do as Christ did in our everyday lives. And that can happen only when we focus on him, become passionate about him, and practice living the way he did.

Details of theology may seem tedious or even boring, but none of us should yawn when we say, "Jesus is Lord." Others may spend hours drawing prophecy charts, but every one of us must draw on the power and wisdom of the One whose future reign over all is certain. It's good to bring our well-developed gifts to whatever we do in the world, but we must know and love the Giver of those gifts. We all have different "minors" in the university of discipleship, but every believer must major on Jesus.

To that end, the rest of this book—parts 2 and 3—focuses on Jesus' life and teachings. This section covers the preparations God made to send his Son into the world and continues with discussions of the means and meat of his message. Through these pages you'll discover anew the Messiah of Scripture and perhaps even revise some of your views of him. You'll take important steps toward a more accurate knowledge of—and stronger connection with—the incomparable Jesus.

JESUS, THE GOD-MAN

PERSONAL STUDY: Matthew 5–6
SCRIPTURE MEMORY: Matthew 26:41;
Philippians 2:5–7
ON YOUR OWN: Background on the Gospels

"A man who was merely a man and said the sort of things Jesus said would not be a great moral teacher. He would either be a lunatic—on the level with the man who says he is a poached egg—or else he would be the Devil of Hell. You must make your choice. Either this man was, and is, the Son of God, or else a madman or something worse."

—C. S. LEWIS

They Said He's Coming (the Prophecies)

Many Christians don't appreciate or understand the vital connection between the Old Testament and the New Testament. For example, there are more than 300 prophecies in the Old Testament that refer specifically to the life of Christ! All of these prophecies came about just as predicted. This is especially amazing when you consider that more than twenty different authors wrote them during a thousand-year period.

The probability of one person fulfilling just eight of the Old Testament prophecies is one in ten to the seventeenth power, or one in 100,000,000,000,000,000 (one hundred million billion). The likelihood of accidentally fulfilling just forty-eight prophecies is one in 100 to the 157th power. Jesus fulfilled them all.

These prophecies tell us a lot about Jesus. Through the prophets, God revealed many facts about Jesus' birth, life, and death. These signposts not only point to the Savior but also serve as proof of the divine origin of Scripture and confirm the divine nature of Jesus. To begin our study, we will look up several prophecies and their fulfillment in the life of Christ.

The Fulfillment of Prophecy

Read the following passages to see the correlation between the Old Testament prophecy and its fulfillment in the New Testament. Write down how Jesus fulfilled each prophecy.

1. What was unique about Jesus' birth (see Isaiah 7:14; Matthew 1:18–25), and where was he predicted to be born (see Micah 5:2; Matthew 2:1–6)?

2. How would Jesus be honored (see Psalm 72:10–11; Isaiah 60:6; Matthew 2:11)?

3. Where would Jesus live as a young child (see Hosea 11:1; Matthew 2:14–15)? Where would he minister when he grew up (see Isaiah 9:1–2; Matthew 4:12–16)?

4. What amazing feats would Jesus perform (see Isaiah 35:5–6; Matthew 11:4–5; 15:30–31)?

5. How would Jesus teach (see Psalm 78:2; Matthew 13:34–35)?

6. How would others receive Jesus (see Isaiah 53:3; John 8:48)?

7. For what price would Jesus be betrayed (see Psalm 41:9; Zechariah 11:12–13; Matthew 27:3–10)?

8. How would Jesus die (see Psalm 22:14–18; Matthew 27:33–50; John 19:17–18, 23–24, 28)?

9. What small detail about Jesus' crucifixion would be yet another confirmation of the accuracy of prophecy (see Psalm 34:20; John 19:32–36)? What would Jesus' death accomplish (see Isaiah 53:4–6; 2 Corinthians 5:21)?

10. How would Jesus be buried (see Isaiah 53:9; Matthew 27:57–60)? What would happen to Jesus' body (see Psalm 16:9–10; Acts 2:29–32)?

The Value of Prophecy

11. Which of the prophecies about Christ has made the most significant impression on you in this study?

12. Why is fulfilled prophecy important to Christianity? How does fulfilled prophecy give you more confidence in God?

Our Understanding of Jesus

Think for a moment about a current political figure. What is your opinion of that person? Do other people agree with you? Chances are that every person you meet will have a different perspective. In much the same way, just about every person has an opinion of Jesus. Many believe he was a great teacher. Some believe he was a humble philosopher whose followers altered and then propagated his ideas. Some believe he was our Savior. Some believe he rose from the dead; many do not.

A variety of mistaken ideas about who Jesus Christ actually was still float around. As Christians, we have a special responsibility to get a clear and accurate view of Christ. Jesus is at the center of our faith; he—not our moral code, church, or beliefs—is what people reject when they reject Christianity. We are not just "God-ians," but "Christians." What's more, our understanding of Jesus determines how we interact with him, how we respond to him, and—in the end—whether we spend eternity with him. The first step in being true Christians, then, is to understand who Jesus is.

At the core of Jesus' identity is the truth that he—unlike any human being who has ever lived—is both fully divine and fully human. Throughout church history, heretics have denied one or the other aspect of his nature. This next section will help you understand his dual nature and the implications for you.

Jesus' Eternal Existence

13. What similarities and differences do you observe in Genesis 1:1–3 and John 1:1–3? Why do you think John mimics the language of Genesis as he begins his gospel?

14. What is Jesus' relationship to the creation (see Colossians 1:15–19)? What did Jesus himself claim about his existence (see John 8:58)?

15. When did Jesus share the Father's glory (see John 17:5)? Why is this significant?

16. What is the significance of the phrase Jesus used to describe himself in Revelation 1:8, 17, and 22:12–13?

Jesus' Divinity

17. Even more important than Jesus' preexistence (his life in heaven before he came to earth), the Bible also identifies Jesus as part of the one and only God. He is the second person of the Trinity. What do you understand the Trinity to mean?

18. How is Jesus related to God the Father (see John 10:30)? What divine qualities does he have (see Hebrews 1:2–3)?

19. What is Jesus' relationship to the angels (see Hebrews 1:4–6)? What qualities does Jesus have that belong only to God (see Hebrews 1:8–12)?

Jesus' Humanity

20. In order to come to earth, what was Jesus required to do (see Philippians 2:7–8)?

21. Note that Jesus experienced common human emotions and limitations, including:
- Fatigue (see John 4:6)
- Thirst (see John 4:7)
- Anger (see John 2:14–17)
- Limited knowledge while on earth (see Matthew 24:36)
- Temptation (see Luke 4:2)
- Sadness (see John 11:35)
- A fully human body (see John 1:14)

Why is a fully human Jesus just as important as a fully divine Jesus?

The Importance of Jesus' Identity

22. How does it help us to know that Jesus is fully God (see Hebrews 4:13–14)?

23. How does it help us to know that Jesus is fully human (see Hebrews 4:15–16)?

24. What bearing does our belief about Jesus have on our salvation (see John 8:24)?

Jesus' uniqueness was completely unself-conscious. He didn't need to draw attention to it. It was a fact so obvious to him that it didn't need emphasizing. It was implied rather than asserted.

- Everyone else was a lost sheep; he had come as the Good Shepherd to seek and to save them.
- Everyone else was sick with the disease of sin; he was the doctor who had come to heal them.
- Everyone else was trapped in the darkness of sin and ignorance; he was the light of the world.
- Everyone else was a sinner; he was born to be their Savior and would die for the forgiveness of their sins.
- Everyone else was hungry; he was the bread of life.
- Everyone else was dead in wrongdoing and sin; he could be their life now and their resurrection in the future.

All these metaphors express the moral uniqueness of which he was clearly conscious.

It is this paradox which is so amazing, this combination of the self-centeredness of his teaching and the unself-centeredness of his behavior.

- In thought he put himself first; in deed last.
- He exhibited both the greatest self-esteem and the greatest self-sacrifice.
- He knew himself to be the Lord of all, but he became their servant.
- He said that he would one day come to judge the world, but he washed the feet of his friends.

This utter disregard of self in the service of God and man is what the Bible calls love.

—JOHN STOTT, *Basic Christianity*

Your Walk with God

Bible

Schedule three times this week to be alone with God. Each day, read the passage indicated below and answer the questions that follow.

DAY ONE: MATTHEW 5:1–30

Some of the things I observe in this passage:

One idea for how to apply this passage to my life:

DAY TWO: MATTHEW 5:31–6:4

Some of the things I observe in this passage:

One idea for how to apply this passage to my life:

DAY THREE: MATTHEW 6:5–34

Some of the things I observe in this passage:

One idea for how to apply this passage to my life:

Prayer

On each of your three days with God this week, pray for the following:

Day One (Adoration): Using Psalm 119, worship God for the trustworthiness of his Word. Then identify one truth in Matthew 6 for which you can praise and thank God.

Day Two (Confession): Read Hebrews 12:1–4. What do you learn from these verses about your struggle with sin? Look up Matthew 26:41 and pray for help in an area of frequent temptation in your life.

Day Three (Supplication): Call one person from the group—make it a surprise—and find out what were his or her three major requests from last week so you can pray for him or her.

Scripture Memory

Memorize these verses this week:

> *"Watch and pray so that you will not fall into temptation. The spirit is willing, but the flesh is weak"* (Matthew 26:41).

> *In your relationships with one another, have the same mindset as Christ Jesus: Who, being in very nature God, did not consider equality with God something to be used to his own advantage; rather, he made himself nothing by taking the very nature of a servant, being made in human likeness* (Philippians 2:5–7).

In the next study, we will take a look at the careful preparations God made for the coming of Christ and also the birth and childhood of Jesus. To prepare yourself for the discussion, consider the reasons why God would want to be intimately involved even in matters relating to Jesus' birth and family of origin. What was remarkable to you about Jesus' birth?

On Your Own: Background on the Gospels

The first four books in the New Testament tell about the life of Christ. These are complementary accounts—similar to four newspapers covering the same story, or four books about the same famous person. Each stands alone as an account of the life of Christ, and though they contain many of the same stories and teachings, they were directed to different audiences and written by different authors. Here are some of the similarities and differences between them.

Gospel of Matthew

THE AUTHOR:

- One of the original twelve disciples, also called Levi
- Is mentioned in four lists of the Twelve (see Matthew 10:3; Mark 3:18; Luke 6:15; Acts 1:13)
- Was called to follow Jesus (see Matthew 9:9–13; Mark 2:14–17; Luke 5:27–32)
- Was a tax collector for the Romans
- Wrote his gospel around AD 70

THE BOOK:

- Matthew wrote specifically to Jews and emphasized Jesus as king.
- His purpose was to show the Jews that Jesus fulfilled Old Testament prophecy.
- He presented Jesus' teaching topically and contrasted Jesus with the Pharisees—the Jewish religious experts of the day.

Gospel of Mark

THE AUTHOR:

- Was a close companion of Peter; told his story through the eyes of Peter
- Full name was John Mark
- Was the son of a Mary whose house was a meeting place for the disciples (see Acts 12:12)
- Was possibly converted as a result of Peter's ministry; is mentioned in 2 Timothy 4:11
- Was a cousin of Barnabas
- Wrote his gospel around AD 60

THE BOOK:

- Mark wrote mainly to the Romans and emphasized Jesus as servant.
- He recorded Jesus' actions more than his teaching and concentrated on Jesus' power and authority.

Gospel of Luke

THE AUTHOR:

- Is mentioned only three times in the New Testament: Colossians 4:14 (called "the doctor"), Philemon 24 (Paul's "fellow worker"), and 2 Timothy 4:11 (with Paul right before his death)
- Was a Gentile (non-Jew)
- Was a companion of Paul on his second and third missionary journeys
- Was in Caesarea from AD 58 to 60 while Paul was in prison; since Jerusalem was only a few miles from Caesarea, this would have given him the opportunity to collect firsthand data about Jesus
- Wrote his gospel around AD 80

THE BOOK:

- Luke addressed his gospel to "Theophilus."
- It was written to the Greeks, or Gentiles (non-Jews), and emphasized Jesus' humanity.
- Luke's gospel is scholarly and historical, dealing with human needs (such as the weak, the suffering, and the outcast) and presents the human side of the Son of God.
- It is really part of a two-volume set, the second being "the book of Acts," which tells the story of the early church.

Gospel of John

THE AUTHOR:

- Isn't identified until the end of the book, where he calls himself the "disciple whom Jesus loved" (see John 21:20, 24)
- Father's name was Zebedee (see Matthew 4:21)
- Mother seems to have been Salome (see Matthew 27:56; Mark 15:40); she may have been the sister of the Mary who was the mother of Jesus (if so, John was Jesus' cousin and could have known him since childhood)
- Was a fisherman
- Was one of the three inner-circle disciples
- Also wrote three epistles (1, 2, and 3 John) and Revelation
- Wrote his gospel around AD 90

THE BOOK:

- The gospel of John is directed to a general audience and emphasizes the deity of Christ.
- It consists mainly of Jesus' discussions and conversations.
- John's purpose in writing is spelled out in 20:31: *"These are written that you may believe that Jesus is the Messiah, the Son of God, and that by believing you may have life in his name."*

THE EARLY YEARS

PERSONAL STUDY: Matthew 7–8

SCRIPTURE MEMORY: Hebrews 1:1–2

ON YOUR OWN: John the Baptist, the Wise Men, and King Herod

"The Son of God became a man to enable men to become sons of God."

—C. S. LEWIS

Countdown to His Coming

When you were in school, you probably preferred the teachers who showed personal interest in you—the ones who called you by your first name and talked with you on a personal level. It's likely the ones who simply lectured from the front and didn't connect with you in any way are just a dim memory. We simply don't respond well to teachers who refuse to enter our personal worlds, no matter how important the lesson they may convey to us.

In keeping his promise to send the Messiah, God went far beyond teaching a message; he became personally involved in the lives of individual people. He used a real live pair of newlyweds named Mary and Joseph to be the parents of his Son, even to the point of sending angels to tell them what would happen and to warn them of dangers. Through these personal visits, he protected and guided them. God did not merely fulfill prophecy himself but also allowed others to participate in the sovereign plan he was unfolding.

In this study, you will see how God prepared the way for Jesus to be born into the world and how this involvement demonstrates his ongoing desire to be personally involved in your life today. You will also see God's faithfulness in the events that surrounded the birth and childhood of Jesus.

The First Promise: John the Baptist

1. How would you describe Zechariah and Elizabeth (see Luke 1:5–7)?

2. In your own words, what happened to Zechariah in Luke 1:8–13?

3. What do you learn about John the Baptist from this account (see Luke 1:13–17)?

4. How did Zechariah and Elizabeth respond to this good news (see Luke 1:18–25)?

5. What can you learn about your own responses to God from this story?

The Second Promise: Christ Himself

6. What was the angel's message to Mary (see Luke 1:26–38)?

7. How did Joseph respond to the situation in which he found himself (see Matthew 1:18–25)?

8. What were some of the similarities in the circumstances of John the Baptist's and Jesus' births? What were the significant differences?

9. What lessons do Mary and Joseph's experience provide for you today?

The Promises Fulfilled

10. What was the focus of Mary and Elizabeth's conversation in Luke 1:39–45?

11. As you read Mary's song of praise in Luke 1:45–55, what does Mary say about God that is just as true today as it was then?

12. What did Mary say about God that especially applies to a need in your life? How could that statement help you?

Jesus' Birth and Childhood

Many people regard the Christmas story as a marvelous, heartwarming event—but one that has little relevance for understanding the life and mission of Jesus while he was on earth. To them, it is mere background or historical details—or, worse, they treat it like a fable. What a shame! Because they haven't grasped the tremendous work that God accomplished at Jesus' birth and in his childhood, they find it difficult to apply this portion of the Gospels to their lives.

But the events surrounding the life of Christ tell us what *happens*, not only what *happened*. The challenge for you is to ask what these events reveal about the character of God. By telling you about what God *did*, they will show you what God does *now*. Although his specific actions may vary throughout history, his character will always be consistent—faithful, powerful, sovereign, and caring.

The Birth of John the Baptist

13. What was the controversy surrounding John's name (see Luke 1:57–66)?

14. What does Zechariah and Elizabeth's insistence on naming their baby *John* tell us about their character (see Luke 1:13)?

15. What were the results of Zechariah's obedience (see Luke 1:63–67)?

16. What can you learn from this passage that applies to your life today?

The Birth of Jesus

17. What additional light did Paul shed on Jesus' birth in Romans 5:6 and Galatians 4:4?

18. What do we learn in Matthew 1:19 about the kind of man Joseph was?

19. How might your response to the angel's announcement of Jesus' birth in Luke 2:8–20 have been similar to the shepherds' reaction?

20. What was the significance of Mary's reaction to the events surrounding Jesus' birth (see Luke 2:17–19)?

Jesus' Infancy and Childhood

21. Why do you think God drew the magi to visit Jesus (see Matthew 2:1–12)?

22. How did Jesus spend his early childhood (see Matthew 2:13–23)?

23. What do we know about Jesus' later childhood (see Luke 2:39–52)?

Your Walk with God

Bible

Schedule three times this week to be alone with God. Each day, read the passage indicated below and answer the questions that follow.

DAY ONE: MATTHEW 7:1–20

Some of the things I observe in this passage:

One idea for how to apply this passage to my life:

DAY TWO: MATTHEW 7:21–8:13

Some of the things I observe in this passage:

One idea for how to apply this passage to my life:

DAY THREE: MATTHEW 8:14–34

Some of the things I observe in this passage:

One idea for how to apply this passage to my life:

Prayer

On each of your three days with God this week, pray for the following:

Day One (Adoration): Pray using Psalm 113 as a guide. Identify five specific aspects of creation that point to God's creativity and thank him for them. In order to observe them firsthand, go for a walk and pray as you go.

Day Two (Confession): What progress are you seeing in the area of temptation with which you struggle? To what do you attribute this growth? If you are not seeing any progress, why do you think this is the case?

Day Three (Supplication): Write out a prayer about three major concerns in your life. When you are finished, be still for a few moments in God's presence, listening to him. Write down what he is impressing on you.

Scripture Memory

Memorize these verses this week:

> *In the past God spoke to our ancestors through the prophets at many times
> and in various ways, but in these last days he has spoken to us by his Son,
> whom he appointed heir of all things, and through whom also he made the
> universe* (Hebrews 1:1–2).

The next study will focus on Satan's temptation of Christ in the wilderness and
the message of salvation that Jesus brought to the world. To prepare, think about
the greatest areas of temptation that you face at this time. What do you do to resist
temptation? What do you consider the main message of Jesus to be?

On Your Own: John the Baptist, the Wise Men, and King Herod

Who Was John the Baptist?

One of the most colorful characters in the New Testament is John the Baptist. John
lived in the wilderness under rugged conditions. His appearance was striking, even
strange. We read that his clothes were made of camel's hair and that he ate locusts
and wild honey. But John made God's righteousness a public issue. His message
could be summed up by the theme "repent and live righteously." He challenged
those secure in their religious attitudes to abandon their sin or face judgment. By
doing so, he prepared the way for the One who would embody righteousness and
deliver those who turned to God from that coming judgment.

John the Baptist was certainly an unusual person, but his life and message had
a positive effect on the people of his day. He took a stand; he was a man of con-
victions; he promised new life through repentance; and he lived continuously filled
with God's Spirit. These and other qualities compelled the masses to hold him in
high esteem.

Just as John the Baptist paved the way for the Messiah on earth back then, the
account of his life and actions can make a highway to prepare you for the work
of Jesus in your life today. There is a fine line between the truth that attracts and

differences that repel! For many Christians, being different means being odd. Some "major on minors." In other words, they mark themselves by what they don't do: no smoking, no drinking, no card playing, and so on.

Such behavior, however, isn't necessarily an indication of true spirituality. It is far better to develop an internal character that stands out. The watching world may then come to say, "Christians are people who are compassionate and generous, who serve others, and who are role models for upright living." They will say "Christians *are*" rather than "Christians *don't*."

What about you? Do people perceive you as different . . . in an attractive way? Remember the kind of difference that brings people to God is found in the lives of servants such as John the Baptist.

Who Were the Wise Men?

The wise men were students of the stars, or astrologers, who probably came from Persia (modern-day Iran). Because the Jews were at one time under Persian rule, the Persians probably were familiar with the religion of the Jews and their messianic hopes.

In seeking out the newborn king, the wise men's first stop was not Bethlehem but Jerusalem. They checked in with King Herod, naively assuming that he and his court would be excited about the Messiah. Herod was excited—but not in the way the wise men assumed. Insecure and treacherous, Herod planned to kill the child and eliminate a future rival. He asked the wise men to report back to him when they had found the Christ child so he could "worship" him too. But the wise men were warned in a dream not to go back to Herod and returned to their country via a different route.

Even though the wise men were not Jews, they were quick to realize the majesty and significance of Jesus' birth. They presented him valuable treasure and worshiped him. Their arrival was a foreshadowing of the good news that God wanted all people—regardless of race, culture, or religious heritage—to be included in his kingdom. These men had nothing but their belief in Jesus. That was exactly what pleased God then, and it still pleases him today!

Who Was King Herod?

The Romans had given Herod the title of "King of the Jews," but the people had never accepted him as their king. Herod was consumed by worries over his own position and power. He had ten wives over the years, two of whom he had killed. He also killed three of his own sons, plus his brother-in-law and one of his wife's grandfathers. The news about the baby born to be king threatened his already shaky security. Knowing this about his nature and character helps us to understand why he ordered all baby boys under the age of two to be killed.

THE MESSAGE

PERSONAL STUDY: Matthew 9–11
SCRIPTURE MEMORY: 1 Corinthians 10:13; John 3:16
ON YOUR OWN: The Kingdom of God

"The essence of love is self-sacrifice. Even the worst of us is adorned by an occasional flash of such nobility, but the life of Jesus radiated it with a never-fading incandescent glow. Jesus was sinless because he was selfless. Such selflessness is love. And God is love."

—John Stott

The Temptation of Jesus

We all struggle with temptation. The specific temptations each of us faces differs from person to person, but none of us escapes all of them. And whether or not we ask God to save us from it, it always returns. We seem never to be done with our evil desires.

What can we do about temptation? Centuries ago Martin Luther said, "You cannot keep birds from flying over your head, but you can keep them from building a nest in your hair!" Temptations, like birds in the air, will always be with us. But we should not, nor do we have to, allow them to "roost." We can resist.

Jesus faced temptation countless times, and we can learn a great deal about how to resist from the way he resisted. We have one story in which he resisted temptation just before his public ministry began. After fasting for forty days, the devil came personally and presented three temptations aimed right at Jesus' human weaknesses. The way Jesus resisted can teach us how to keep sin from "roosting" in our lives.

The First Temptation

1. *Read Matthew 3:13–4:11.* What were the circumstances surrounding Jesus' time of temptation (see Matthew 3:13–17)?

2. What did Satan first tempt Jesus to do (see Matthew 4:3–4)?

3. What would be tempting about suggesting that Jesus miraculously make bread?

4. Why would it have been wrong for Jesus to give in to Satan's temptation?

5. How did Jesus respond (see Matthew 4:4)?

6. How can you imitate Jesus' example of resisting temptation?

The Second Temptation

7. What was the second temptation Jesus faced (see Matthew 4:5–7)?

8. Why would it have been wrong for Jesus to give in to Satan's temptation?

9. How did Jesus respond (see Matthew 4:7)?

The Third Temptation

10. What was the third temptation Satan tried on Jesus (see Matthew 4:8–10)?

11. What was the significance of this temptation?

12. How did Jesus respond (see Matthew 4:10)?

What We Can Learn

13. What do you learn about Satan's tactics from this story?

14. What can you learn about resisting temptation from Jesus' example?

The Message Jesus Brought

It was many years ago, but you're sure you could get there again if you had to. You went to that quaint little restaurant on your honeymoon . . . how could you forget? And now you've just told a friend who's visiting the same area to be sure to go there. You've given him directions, confident your recollections accurately describe the way to get to the best seafood in town.

Confident, that is, until you get a call from your friend, who tells you the roads don't go the way you recollected. He has gone forty-five minutes out of his way because he trusted in the map you drew from your memory. You hang up the phone, wondering how you could have been so certain when you were so certainly wrong.

Many people think they have the facts straight about the Gospels and the identity of Jesus, but when they actually delve into the message of the New Testament, they realize several of their cherished ideas need serious revision. In the gospel of John, we encounter one such man who thought he understood God's ways but had to encounter the reality of his erroneous thinking. Nicodemus was not an atheist, but a religious teacher—someone familiar with the Scriptures. In some ways, he was like many people today who are religious but misinformed—people who need the new birth from heaven brought by the Spirit.

Jesus' statements to Nicodemus put the gospel message, the basic message of salvation, into a clear and concise package. We should turn to this story as a model of how the gospel should be shared with others.

Jesus' Talk with Nicodemus

15. *Read John 3:1–4.* What do we know about Nicodemus (see John 3:1–2)?

16. How do we know that Nicodemus respected Jesus (see John 3:2)?

17. How did Jesus answer Nicodemus' words (see John 3:3)?

18. What did Nicodemus misunderstand about Jesus saying that he had to be "born again" (John 3:4)?

Jesus' Talk with the Woman at the Well

19. *Read John 4:1–26.* What details do we learn about the woman Jesus met (see John 4:4–8, 17–18)?

20. How did Jesus answer the woman's first question (see John 4:9–10)?

21. What truth did Jesus want the woman to understand (see John 4:10–14, 25–26)?

Jesus' Main Message

22. How would you summarize Jesus' main message (see John 3:16; 4:13–14)?

Your Walk with God

Bible

Schedule three times this week to be alone with God. Each day, read the passage indicated below and answer the questions that follow.

DAY ONE: MATTHEW 9

Some of the things I observe in this passage:

One idea for how to apply this passage to my life:

DAY TWO: MATTHEW 10

Some of the things I observe in this passage:

One idea for how to apply this passage to my life:

DAY THREE: MATTHEW 11

Some of the things I observe in this passage:

One idea for how to apply this passage to my life:

Prayer

On each of your three days with God this week, pray for the following:

Day One (Adoration): Make a list of answers to these questions: (1) How has God shown his love for you recently? (2) How has God shown patience to you? Praise God for each one.

Day Two (Confession): Paraphrase Psalm 51:1–9, putting it in words that speak directly to you, and use it as a guide for your prayer.

Day Three (Supplication): What are the three greatest needs in your life right now? Pray about those needs.

Scripture Memory

Memorize these verses this week:

> *No temptation has overtaken you except what is common to mankind. And God is faithful; he will not let you be tempted beyond what you can bear. But when you are tempted, he will also provide a way out so that you can endure it* (1 Corinthians 10:13).

For God so loved the world that he gave his one and only Son, that whoever believes in him shall not perish but have eternal life (John 3:16).

Next week we will study about those who followed Jesus—the disciples—and examine Christ's teachings in the Sermon on the Mount. To prepare, ask yourself who Jesus wanted his disciples to be and what you think Jesus expects of a disciple today. Also write down a wise saying or quote that provided direction or comfort in your life at some point.

On Your Own: The Kingdom of God

Contrary to popular belief, Jesus' mission wasn't to teach us how to become better people. He didn't come to make us *nice*; he came to bring us *life*. He taught that we are all dead spiritually and must be born again into the kingdom of God. A new set of "to dos" just wouldn't cut it!

Jesus spoke more about the kingdom of God than about any other subject. He said it exists here on earth, though it is "hidden" in the midst of the world we see (see Matthew 13:44). He said that while human beings lead earthly kingdoms and create structures to control our behaviors, God's kingdom has no human leader and is about changing hearts and minds from within.

Jesus told people they needed to die to self, not just turn over a new leaf. He said those who wanted to be the first in his kingdom would appear to be the last by worldly standards (see Matthew 20:16). He told people his kingdom was of utmost value in life, but that, paradoxically, it was available to all who simply asked to be included. Although Jesus told people to keep seeking, asking, and knocking on the door to find truth (see Matthew 7:7), he emphasized that it was God who was more actively seeking them—that God was always on a quest to bring in lost people like a shepherd goes after lost sheep (see Luke 15:1–7).

Heaven Can Wait

We sometimes think of God's kingdom as heaven—a place where, if we believe in Jesus and trust him to forgive our sins, we will go when we die. Yet on the whole,

Jesus stressed living with him *now*, not just someday after we die. We are to build our earthly lives on his teaching and engage in fulfilling his mission—not just wait around for death (see Matthew 7:24). The very moment we are born again, we begin our eternal life with him. Jesus' central message was an invitation into that life not someday, but right now.

In John 3, Jesus tells Nicodemus that in order to see the kingdom of God, a person must be born again. A few verses later, John adds the summary of Jesus' message: "For God so loved the world that he gave his one and only Son, that whoever believes in him shall not perish but have eternal life" (John 3:16). By trusting in him, we can have that life now. Jesus wants us to be "all in"—to align every thought, word, and deed to his ways. "Not everyone who says to me, 'Lord, Lord,' will enter the kingdom of heaven, but only the one who does the will of my Father who is in heaven" (Matthew 7:21).

The Kingdom Is Here

Jesus would often proclaim to people that the kingdom of God was "near" or "among them" or "at hand." On one occasion, when the Pharisees asked Jesus when the kingdom of God would come, he replied, "The coming of the kingdom of God is not something that can be observed, nor will people say, 'Here it is,' or 'There it is,' because the kingdom of God is in your midst" (Luke 17:20–21). An alternate translation is "the kingdom of God is within you."

Jesus thus taught an important aspect of the kingdom of God: it is a way to reorder our inner world that then impacts our outer world. He called us to a change of heart that transforms our actions. When our inner world is ruled by the King, the kingdom is indeed at hand. In that realm, God's love for us inspires us to love our neighbors—and even our enemies (see Matthew 5:44). Such a change of heart leads us to care for "the least of these," including the hungry, the sick, and even prisoners (see Matthew 25:31–46).

The kingdom of God doesn't reside in some neat little corner of our lives. We cannot cut up our lives and label one slice as "spiritual." Jesus isn't interested in our spiritual life—he's interested in *our whole life!* God's kingdom impacts every aspect of who we are and what we do, much like yeast works its way through a lump of dough (see Matthew 13:33).

Jesus' invitation to enter his kingdom is an invitation to be a part of the work of God right now, right here, wherever we are. It is an invitation to live life to the full, now and forever.

THE MISSION

PERSONAL STUDY: Matthew 12; 15:31–50
SCRIPTURE MEMORY: 1 Corinthians 9:24
ON YOUR OWN: Seek and Save the Lost

"Jesus asked only that His disciples follow Him. Knowledge was not communicated by the Master in terms of laws and dogmas, but in the living personality of One who walked among them. His disciples were distinguished, not by outward conformity to certain rituals, but by being with Him."
—ROBERT E. COLEMAN, *THE MASTER PLAN OF EVANGELISM*

Jesus Selects His Team

The starting gun goes off. The crowd of runners surges forward. The spectators cheer. The TV cameras record the early leaders, and the sports commentators tell us about those who have begun well.

But this is a *marathon,* not a sprint. Once the initial excitement of the start wears off, we become distracted by something else. Later in the day, we'll turn back to see who wins. Only at the finish line will the thrill of the start be matched—and exceeded. What happens in between usually is of little interest to the spectators. Yet that is where the race is won or lost.

The Christian life is like a marathon. Many enter and even start well, but it's hard to tell who's going to hang in there. Some get distracted or lack the endurance to finish. Others are deceived by their own confidence and get tripped up because they weren't cautious. Those who finish the race have disciplined their minds and bodies. They aren't sprinters, but long-distance runners. When the tedium and pain of the mid-race are almost unbearable, they persevere. They are the ones who finish well.

Jesus called the apostles to a marathon that we also know as *discipleship*. Some of them started well. Some of them tripped up along the way. One left the race— never to enter again. But Jesus wanted all of them to follow him . . . for the long haul. The purpose of this study is to learn from the experience of the disciples that Jesus wants us to follow him for life.

Jesus' Disciples Back Then

1. What considerations did Jesus likely weigh when selecting the twelve apostles (see Luke 6:12–16)?

2. Why is it significant that Jesus called the apostles to "be with him" (Mark 3:14)?

3. What were Peter and Andrew doing when Jesus called them? How did they respond to his invitation to follow him (see Matthew 4:18–20)?

4. Who else did Jesus call to follow him that same day (see Matthew 4:21–22)?

5. How is Matthew (also called Levi) described in Mark 2:13–17? How did the Pharisees react when Jesus called him to be his follower?

6. What happened to the twelve apostles by the time Jesus left the earth (see Acts 1:21–26)?

Jesus' Disciples Today

7. What initially attracted you to Jesus? Why did you intially become a Christian?

8. Why do you still follow Jesus?

9. Some of Jesus' disciples stopped following him after a while (see John 6:66–71). What causes Christians to give up following Christ?

10. What are some of the benefits of staying faithful to Christ?

11. What do you need to do to be a better disciple?

The New Attitudes

What would you do if you were turned down for a lucrative job after weeks of grueling interviews? Would you sit back, become depressed, and blame yourself for not being a more dynamic person? Or would you take the setback in stride and look forward to the next opportunity? It all depends on your *attitude*. The attitudes that shape your actions will go a long way in determining the quality of your friendships, your performance at your job, and your service for God. In a very real way, attitude is everything.

Attitude is the central theme of one of the most famous passages in all of Scripture: the Sermon on the Mount found in Matthew 5–7. The Sermon on the Mount is central to Jesus' teaching, for it summarizes the characteristics of those who know God personally. In this sermon, Jesus instructs us on how we ought to live and who we ought to be. It is a message he gave repeatedly as he traveled from place to place.

This study covers Matthew 5:1–16, the section of the Sermon on the Mount in which Jesus describes believers' new attitudes, or "Beatitudes," as they're often called. You will learn several ways in which Jesus wants your attitudes and actions to be different from those of the world.

The Beatitudes

12. What does it mean to be poor in spirit (see Matthew 5:3)?

13. What should you mourn over (see Matthew 5:4)?

14. What does it mean to be meek (see Matthew 5:5)?

15. Why is it important for you to desire righteousness (see Matthew 5:6)?

16. Why is it important to show mercy to others (see Matthew 5:7)?

17. What is purity in heart (see Matthew 5:8)?

18. What does it mean to be a "peacemaker" (see Matthew 5:9)?

19. Why are righteous people sometimes persecuted (see Matthew 5:10–12)?

The Beatitudes vs. the World's Attitudes

20. Fill in the blanks from your own experience:

JESUS SAYS	THE WORLD SAYS
Blessed are the poor in spirit.	
Blessed are those who mourn.	
Blessed are the meek.	
Blessed are those who hunger and thirst for righteousness.	
Blessed are the merciful.	
Blessed are the pure in heart.	
Blessed are the peacemakers.	
Blessed are those who are persecuted because of righteousness.	

Your Walk with God

Bible

Schedule three times this week to be alone with God. Each day, read the passage indicated below and answer the questions that follow.

DAY ONE: MATTHEW 12:1–14

Some of the things I observe in this passage:

One idea for how to apply this passage to my life:

DAY TWO: MATTHEW 12:15–30

Some of the things I observe in this passage:

One idea for how to apply this passage to my life:

DAY THREE: MATTHEW 12:31–50

Some of the things I observe in this passage:

One idea for how to apply this passage to my life:

Prayer

On each of your three days with God this week, pray for the following:

Day One (Adoration): How has God shown his grace (undeserved favor) to you recently? In what recent situations have you clearly seen God's wisdom? Thank him for these things in your life.

Day Two (Confession): Paraphrase Psalm 51:10–19 so that it reflects you and your circumstances. Use it as a guide for your prayer.

Day Three (Thanksgiving): Identify some specific answers to prayer, and list five things related to your family for which you are thankful.

Scripture Memory

Memorize this verse this week:

> *Do you not know that in a race all the runners run, but only one gets the prize? Run in such a way as to get the prize* (1 Corinthians 9:24).

Next week, we will continue our study of the Sermon on the Mount and explore some of Jesus' parables. Take some time to consider your motives for your behavior. Why is it so difficult to have pure motives? Also consider why Jesus told parables when he could have just explained the principles directly.

On Your Own: Seek and Save the Lost

Why did Jesus come to earth? You've been reading this week about his miraculous healings, his brilliant teaching, and his challenge to the religious status quo. But these were all part of a larger mission, which was to do for all of us what we could not do for ourselves. Jesus came to save us by dying on the cross, and then came back from the grave to furnish proof that he was the Son of God and had accomplished his mission.

The tragedy of humanity is that our sin separates us from God. It is a gap that cannot be bridged by good works, religion, or any other human effort. Jesus' death—in which he received the punishment we deserved—restores us to God. This is what theologians call "substitutionary atonement." Jesus, who was without sin, was the substitute sacrifice for our sins. Through his death, and subsequent defeat of death through his resurrection, we are made right with God.

It is human nature to downplay the seriousness of our sin. We tell ourselves we're doing okay and that we're basically good people. We may have a vague hope that if we do end up in trouble, God will overlook our faults. But that's a false hope, and it shows we have a skewed view of ourselves . . . and of God. We underestimate our own goodness, and we fail to respect his holiness, justice, and perfection.

Blessed Are the Poor and Mournful

In the Sermon on the Mount, Jesus invites us to drop the facade and see our need for God. "Blessed are the poor in spirit," he says (Matthew 5:3). What does that mean? Can we *try* to be poor in spirit? How would one even do that? But if Jesus is simply calling us to realize the true condition of our hearts—that we *are* poor and it's a good thing to stop kidding ourselves—then the passage makes sense.

When we realize that we really have nothing, spiritually speaking, and are bankrupt when it comes to righteousness, we can begin to receive blessings from God. Without that awareness, we're smug and self-righteous. The sad truth is that we are empty, and when we finally get honest about that fact, God fills us with his goodness. We're not supposed to *try* to be poor in spirit but realize the poverty of spirit that exists. When we view ourselves as empty-handed, we can reach out for God. But when we grasp tightly to what we think is our own righteousness, our hands stay closed. Jesus invites us to let go of our pride, quit fooling ourselves, and receive what only he can give.

In God's kingdom, many things are reversed from how we usually value them: the first are last, the poor are exalted, and the meek inherit the earth. These statements, on the surface, seem contradictory. The meek in our world don't win—they lose. But Jesus has a different message and a different mission. He took the path of humility and invites us to do the same (see Philippians 2:1–11). He invites us to aspire to things such as purity, peacemaking, and a hunger for righteousness—values that stand in sharp contrast to the striving, aggression, and self-centeredness that is commonplace in our world.

Surrender to Win

Jesus calls us to surrender to God. He modeled this through his own surrender that ultimately led him to the cross. By that obedience and setting aside of his own desires, he accomplished the mission his heavenly Father had given him. He calls us to a similar release of our own privilege and pride.

Jesus tells us we're blessed if we're poor, hungry, thirsty, and mourning. He's not asking us to *try* to be those things—he's asking us to be honest about the fact that they *are already true* of us. In the admission of that reality, we find his comfort. When we admit our weakness, Jesus turns it into strength. In the upside-down world of God's kingdom, we gain our lives by being willing to lose them. If we want to be first, we must be willing to be last; if we want to lead, we must do so by first being a servant.

Jesus' mission was to come and serve—and ultimately, his service led to sacrificing himself for our sins. We cannot "improve" on his gift through any of our efforts; we can only receive the gift. Then, in gratitude, we can live as he did: by giving ourselves daily to whatever the Father asks of us, seeking to do good for others whenever we can. In doing that, we "complete" the mission of Jesus—taking his words and example into our world as every generation is commanded to do (see Matthew 28:19–20).

THE PARABLES

PERSONAL STUDY: Matthew 13–14
SCRIPTURE MEMORY: 1 Samuel 16:7; Matthew 6:33
ON YOUR OWN: Jesus' Way of Storytelling

"Parables show us that things are not as they appear. Our tidy, well-packaged ideas about spirituality, faith, and reality shatter when confronted by Christ and the God he represents."

—RONNIE McBRAYER

The Power of Pure Motives

It is easy to judge people by what we see on the surface. Want to know who is the most committed to the church? Just look at who arrives first on Sunday morning and stays the longest. Want to know who reads God's Word faithfully? Just look at the person who brings a well-worn Bible to small group. It is tempting to measure each other by what we see outwardly. It is also easy to judge motives unfairly. In particular, we tend to believe that our motives are pure and to suspect the motives of others.

God is as concerned with our motives as he is with our outward behavior. He cares about why and how we give, not just how much. He is concerned with why we do good, not just that we do it. Outward obedience alone does not impress God. He wants our heart. In this study, we will explore the importance of motives in all we do, look at eight of Jesus' parables from Matthew 13, and examine them closely to discern how to learn from a parable.

Attitudes and Behavior

1. How do inner attitudes and thoughts affect your outward behavior?

2. Why is it difficult to do good deeds in secret?

Motives to Watch

3. *Murder.* What inner feelings or attitudes are identified with the outward behavior of murder (see Matthew 5:21–26)?

4. *Adultery.* Why did Jesus go beyond condemning the act of adultery (see Matthew 5:27–28)? Why do you think Jesus used such extreme imagery to describe how you should resist sin (see Matthew 5:29–30)?

5. *Hatred.* What inner attitude toward enemies did Jesus condemn (see Matthew 5:43–44)? How do you combat the tendency to scorn your enemies (see Matthew 5:43–44)?

6. *Giving.* What do you need to watch out for when doing good works (see Matthew 6:1)? How should you give (see Matthew 6:2–4)?

7. *Praying.* How would you describe prayer that is pleasing to God (see Matthew 6:5–8)?

8. *Fasting.* In what way should you fast (see Matthew 6:16–18)?

9. *Storing up treasures.* What is a spiritual attitude toward material things?

10. *Worry.* Why is it harmful to incessantly worry about having enough material things (see Matthew 6:25–34)?

He Spoke in Parables

A mother sits in a rocking chair, holding a child in her lap and a book so the child can see. As she reads, the child listens in rapt attention. Perhaps you remember having stories read to you. If so, you probably can also remember many details of the stories you heard. Stories have a way of sticking with us over the years.

Pastors always use stories in the form of illustrations in their sermons. You probably can remember a story your pastor told last week more readily than you can remember the main points. That's because our minds retain pictures more easily than words.

Jesus told many stories. He took common, ordinary experiences and used them to explain spiritual truths that he wanted his disciples to put into practice. We call these stories *parables*. Altogether, the Gospels contain thirty-two different parables. They are an important part of what Jesus taught. Thus, if you are to learn from Jesus, you must become a student of the parables that he told.

11. *The Sower and the Seed* (see Matthew 13:1–23). What is the main point of this parable? What is the condition of your "soil"?

12. *The Weeds Among the Wheat* (see Matthew 13:24–30, 36–43). What lesson did Jesus want to communicate in comparing people to weeds and wheat?

13. *The Mustard Seed* (see Matthew 13:31–32). How does the mustard seed illustrate faith?

14. *The Leaven* (see Matthew 13:33). What qualities does yeast possess that would make it a fitting illustration of the kingdom of heaven?

15. *The Hidden Treasure* (see Matthew 13:44). What is the main point of this parable?

16. *The Costly Pearl* (see Matthew 13:45–46). Why is a pearl of great value like the kingdom of heaven?

17. *The Fishing Net* (see Matthew 13:47–50). Why would Jesus compare a fishing net to the kingdom of heaven?

18. *The Unmerciful Servant* (see Matthew 18:21–35). What is the main point of this parable?

Apply It to Your Life

19. Why do you think Jesus used so many parables in his teaching (see Matthew 13:1–23)?

20. Which of the parables in this lesson relates to a concern you have for someone else? Explain your answer.

21. As you look over this study, what motives do you recognize that hinder your relationship with God (see Matthew 6:25–34)?

22. What steps could you take to bring your inner self more in line with God's desire for you?

Your Walk with God

Bible

Schedule three times this week to be alone with God. Each day, read the passage indicated below and answer the questions that follow.

DAY ONE: MATTHEW 13:1–44

Some of the things I observe in this passage:

One idea for how to apply this passage to my life:

DAY TWO: MATTHEW 13:45–14:12

Some of the things I observe in this passage:

One idea for how to apply this passage to my life:

DAY THREE: MATTHEW 14:13–36

Some of the things I observe in this passage:

One idea for how to apply this passage to my life:

Prayer

On each of your three days with God this week, pray for the following:

Day One (Adoration): Go for a walk. Carry on a simple conversation with God that includes elements of adoration, confession, thanksgiving, and supplication. Try talking softly out loud as you walk.

Day Two (Supplication): Say something or do something to encourage someone else. You can write a note, make a phone call, buy a small gift, or make something. Then pray specifically for that person.

Day Three (Confession): Take an inventory of your life. Claim God's forgiveness for any sin you recall. Also respond to the following two questions: (1) What do you need God's power for this week? (2) What do you need God's wisdom for this week?

Scripture Memory

Memorize these verses this week:

> *But the LORD said to Samuel, "Do not consider his appearance or his height, for I have rejected him. The LORD does not look at the things people look at. People look at the outward appearance, but the LORD looks at the heart"* (1 Samuel 16:7).

> *But seek first his kingdom and his righteousness, and all these things will be given to you as well* (Matthew 6:33).

In the next study, we will take a closer look at the compassion that Jesus demonstrated for people and the times when Jesus healed those who were sick. To prepare, consider why some people think that God lacks compassion and whether you believe God still heals people today.

On Your Own: Jesus' Way of Storytelling

Try to recall a talk you heard a month or two ago. How much of it did you retain? Chances are if you remember any of it, you most likely recall the illustrations and anecdotes rather than the points of the message. The same is true of our favorite TV shows, movies, and novels. Years later, we remember the story, not necessarily the specifics of all the dialogue.

Why is that? It's because our brains are hardwired to remember stories. Even when events happen, we remember the stories we make up about those events more than the events themselves. While we can study facts and data and use such information in our everyday lives, there is something about a story that connects to a deeper place in our brain and memory.

The Power of Stories

Good speakers and teachers know their listeners will connect with stories, and they use illustrations, analogies, and drama to convey facts and concepts. They know stories will help their listeners grasp and remember ideas. In the same way, God knows how powerfully stories affect us because he made us that way. So, when he took on human form, he knew exactly how to convey truth to us: through stories.

Jesus taught using parables—brief metaphorical stories. Some parables were short, just a sentence or two; others had more complex plot lines and multiple characters with intriguing, even puzzling, motives. Some of Jesus' parables were like riddles, raising more questions than they answered. Most create vivid images in our minds. Even if we don't understand them, we can retell them.

Simple Stories, Deep Messages

Jesus lived in a culture that was primarily agrarian, so he often talked about the kingdom of God in metaphors to which his first-century culture could relate. He spoke of seeds, vines, sheep, or fields, and the main characters were often farmers, shepherds, or landowners.

Jesus spoke to ordinary people and knew that most of them did not have much formal education. He invited everyone into the kingdom: the poor, the blind, the sick, and those on the fringe. So he told stories to which everyone—even the poor or working-class people—could relate.

Jesus engaged the educated religious leaders in discussion as well. But instead of philosophical debate, he usually told them stories and asked questions. At times they became frustrated, but only because of their stubbornness and pride. Those watching the conversation knew exactly what Jesus was doing and were very much impressed!

Jesus was thus able to engage both the scholars and the ordinary people. In a way, this style of teaching elevated the poor and uneducated, leveling the playing field. They didn't feel excluded because they could relate to and understand stories just as well as religious leaders. Parables broke down the divisions caused by religious elitism.

One of Jesus' most famous parables is called "The Good Samaritan." He told it when challenged by a religious leader to answer the question, "Who is my neighbor?" (see Luke 10:25–37). At the end of the parable, Jesus turned the tables and asked the religious leader a question. He hoped that by inviting the man to say the obvious answer in front of all those watching, the man would see the importance in God's eyes of compassionate action over religious "correctness."

An Invitation to Wrestle with Truth

Parables don't give easy answers, which may be another reason why Jesus used them. Jesus invited people to wrestle with ideas and mull them over. Parables are like expertly cut gemstones, with various facets and angles. We can turn them over, examine them, and notice subtleties that we may have overlooked the first time. They are both simple and complex.

Jesus wasn't inviting people into mere intellectual understanding or even external conformity to rules. He was offering a new life—a transformation of the heart, will, and attitude that would lead to action. Stories and parables sink into a deep place within the human soul. They invite us not just to know a truth but also to live it. A faith-based relationship with God is not based on rules or rote answers. Rather, it is holistic and encompasses all of life. Pondering Jesus' parables takes us more readily into that realm.

As you read the parables of Jesus, you will no doubt appreciate his brilliance and storytelling. But don't stop there. Ask yourself questions that lead to application: *How does this parable touch my heart? Where do I see myself in the story? What is Jesus inviting me to know or do as a result? What attitudes or actions in my life does this story invite me to change?*

THE HEALER

PERSONAL STUDY: Matthew 15; Psalm 23
SCRIPTURE MEMORY: Matthew 11:28
ON YOUR OWN: Scripture Application

"Jesus' miracles are not just a challenge to our minds, but a promise to our hearts, that the world we all want is coming."

—TIM KELLER

Jesus, the Man of Compassion

"You say that God loves the world, but I don't feel it."

"God is out there and I am here, so what does it mean to say I matter to him?"

"Jesus could never love me after the things I've done."

Most people have trouble feeling God's love. Some just don't feel much of anything, so God's love seems meaningless to them. Some are pressed down under the weight of their failures and feel too ashamed and unworthy to embrace God's care. It's difficult to grow in a relationship with God without becoming aware of and accepting his compassion for us. Yet when we understand the depth of God's great tenderness toward us, we are better able to love him back in response.

The purpose of this study is to help you understand the compassionate side of Jesus and show that he did indeed heal those who were sick. You'll learn that Jesus wants to show compassion to those in need—including you—and that you can have confidence in his power to help you during times of need.

Jesus and the Death of Lazarus

1. What was Jesus' response to the news of Lazarus's death (see John 11:33–34)?

2. How did the Jews react when they saw Jesus' emotion (see John 11:35–37)?

3. What does this tell you about Jesus?

Jesus and the Multitudes

4. What events led to the death of John the Baptist (see Matthew 14:3–10)?

5. What does Jesus' response to the death of John the Baptist tell you about how he was feeling (see Matthew 14:13)?

6. When Jesus saw the large crowd that had gathered to see him, how did he view the interruption to his attempt to get away (see Matthew 14:14)?

7. How would you describe the disciples' attitude toward the crowd (see Matthew 14:15)?

8. How did Jesus respond to the disciples' request? What does this show about his attitude toward the people (see Matthew 14:16)?

Jesus and You

9. Think about a time when someone showed compassion toward you. What kind of impact did that person's action have on you?

10. When was a time you showed compassion to someone else? How did that impact you?

Jesus, the Healer

If you moved to a new city, how would you choose your family physician? Chances are you would take into consideration a number of important qualifications. Certainly you would want someone who was knowledgeable and who kept up with the rapid changes in medicine. Just as important, however, would be that doctor's concern for your entire well-being. You would want to sense that this physician genuinely cared about *you* and would want to do everything in his or her power to keep you well or help you get over an illness.

Jesus' healing ministry was a highly personal part of his work. Lest you imagine huge crowds gathered to watch him perform these great miracles, you should keep in mind that he taught the masses but healed individuals. Even when others were looking, he performed healings by touching each person one by one. (The only exception was when he healed ten lepers as a group, but even then they were apart from the crowd.) Remember that one of Satan's temptations was to lure Jesus into using his power to razzle-dazzle potential followers (see Matthew 4:5–6).

Jesus did not use his healing power to draw crowds. He healed people to substantiate his claims and to demonstrate his compassion. He wanted people to be healed, and he also wanted them to understand that he was the one they were waiting for—the Messiah.

Miracles of Healing

11. *Healing the centurion's servant* (see Luke 7:1–10). What facts do you observe about the centurion? What can this story teach about asking Jesus to heal others?

12. *Raising the widow's son* (see Luke 7:11–17). What strikes you about the healing of the widow's son? What does this story teach about Jesus?

13. *Raising Jairus's daughter* (see Mark 5:21–43). Who was Jairus? What can this story teach about trusting God?

14. *Healing of the hemorrhaging woman* (see Mark 5:24–34). What impresses you about the woman Jesus healed? What can this story teach about asking Jesus for help?

15. *Healing of ten lepers* (see Luke 17:11–19). What are some significant details in this healing? What can this story teach about expecting to see results from your prayers?

Apply It to Your Life

16. What general observation can you make from the healings you've studied in this lesson?

17. What do these healings reveal about the nature of Jesus?

18. What is a physical or emotional need you have that these stories can encourage you to bring to God?

Your Walk with God

Bible

Schedule three times this week to be alone with God. Each day, read the passage indicated below and answer the questions that follow.

DAY ONE: MATTHEW 15:1–20

Some of the things I observe in this passage:

One idea for how to apply this passage to my life:

DAY TWO: MATTHEW 15:21–39

Some of the things I observe in this passage:

One idea for how to apply this passage to my life:

DAY THREE: PSALM 23

Some of the things I observe in this passage:

One idea for how to apply this passage to my life:

Prayer

On each of your three days with God this week, pray for the following:

Day One (Adoration): Write down your thoughts to this question: *What does the sending of Jesus tell you about God?* Spend some time praising him.

Day Two (Confession): Go for a walk and use it as a time to "clear the air" between you and the Lord. Think back over the events and conversations of this week. For what do you need to claim God's forgiveness?

Day Three (Thanksgiving): Fill in the following blanks, thanking God for . . .

A spiritual blessing:	
A friendship blessing:	
A family blessing:	
A spouse or relational blessing:	
A material blessing:	

Scripture Memory

Memorize this verse this week:

> *"Come to me, all you who are weary and burdened, and I will give you rest"* (Matthew 11:28).

On Your Own: Scripture Application

Wrong Use of Scripture

Just because we read what someone did or believed in a passage of Scripture, it doesn't mean we know what God wants us to do or believe now. We can misinterpret the passage and get the wrong meaning, or we can get the right meaning but misunderstand what we are to do in our specific situation. The Bible isn't prescriptive in everything it records, because along with commands from God, it records the lies of Satan and the sinful actions of people. Those are actually examples we should *not* follow even though technically they are "taught" in the Bible.

Furthermore, much of the Bible is history. It tells us what happened, but not what should happen. We don't know just from a story if what we read is a pattern of how God will usually act, or if it is a special state of affairs that is not meant to serve as a template for future expectations. When we read someone did something in the Bible, yes—we rightly conclude people did that; and if God is said to have done something, we're right to believe it. But like the Great Flood, God does some things only once; and like the actions of so many biblical characters, they are not necessarily behaviors we should copy.

Here's a silly story that can illustrate how we can misapply Scripture. A foolish person wanted to know from God what he should do. So he "prayed" for guidance and decided to flip open his Bible at random to get direction. "It's all God's Word," he surmised, "so I'll do whatever I read in the text to do!" In his first attempt, he opened the page to Matthew 27:5 and read, "So Judas . . . went away and hanged himself."

Stunned, he thought maybe he should try a different passage, so he flipped over a few pages to Luke 10:37, where he read straight out of the mouth of Jesus, "Go and do likewise." He began to tremble at the thought of what "the Bible was telling him to do," so he thought he'd give it one more try. "Well, Lord," he said, "you wrote in 2 Corinthians 13:1 that 'every matter must be established by the testimony of two or three witnesses,' so here's my third try." He closed his Bible and let it again fall open at random. This time, he landed on John 13:27: "What you are about to do, do quickly."

Out of Context

No one would be that simpleminded, right? But we can come dangerously close to doing what the man did in this story. If we take a passage out of context, we can think we're supposed to do something the text is not telling us to do. Furthermore, if we read about something the children of Israel or the early church did, we shouldn't automatically think that's a pattern for us to follow.

For example, in Acts 5:1–10 we read that Ananias and Sapphira dropped over dead in a church gathering. Should we then expect people routinely to die from God's judgment at our worship services? Is that some kind of "usual and customary" thing God does—the proof of his powerful presence in our midst? Most people would say "no," but there are many other things in the book of Acts that people allege are "pure" practices we ought to recover in our day.

Maybe we should . . . but maybe not! The historical sections of the Bible don't usually include that information. We have to look for repeated actions and patterns and confirm those from didactic and prescriptive sections of Scripture to know if we should "go and do likewise."

Questions for Application

So, when we read the text, we must first take into account the context. We must try to understand the historical setting and where those people were in redemptive history, versus where we are today. We must look for commands that occur more than once so we can have confirmation they apply to all God's people at all times in all places (many do not). Difficult passages must be interpreted in the light of clearer passages. Once we've done that work, we can set about to discover what God might want us to do in our situation.

We must also not make the opposite mistake of reading the text academically. It is not a collection of dead words or a matter of mere human speculation. We are reading God's Word, even if the application will take some work to discover. We approach the text reverently and humbly, inviting the Holy Spirit to illumine it and prepare us to obey.

What are some good application questions to ask? Here is a simple list of questions you can use. They are not foolproof, but using them can take you beyond a dry, lifeless reading of the Bible to a place of informed obedience and exciting experimentation.

- Is there a promise to claim?
- Is there a command to obey?
- Is there sin to confess?
- Is there an example to follow?
- Is there a behavior to change?
- Is there an encouragement to receive?
- Is there an insight to gain?
- Is there an issue to pray about?
- Is there a reason to worship God?

We encourage you to try asking these questions this week as you are reading your Bible assignment. See if they lead to a richer interaction with God's Word.

GETTING TO KNOW JESUS

This review culminates your study of Part 2, *Getting to Know Jesus.* Use this time to reflect on your experience and summarize what you've learned about Christ. It can also be an affirming time to express your appreciation to fellow group members for the growing bond between you. Being a Christian means more than just knowing about Jesus; it means knowing him personally. Your knowledge of Christ should change you. So, as you do this review, spend time sharing how Jesus is changing you.

Reflect on What You've Learned

1. Why is it significant that Jesus fulfilled the prophecies of the Old Testament?

2. Why is it important to affirm that Jesus is both fully God and fully man?

3. What did you learn about resisting temptation from Jesus resisting Satan in the wilderness?

4. What did you learn about ministering to others from the way Jesus selected and nurtured his twelve apostles?

5. How would you summarize Jesus' main message (the gospel)?

6. Which of the Beatitudes did you find the most challenging to apply?

7. Why does religious behavior without the proper motives fail to please God?

8. How do you know that Jesus has compassion on you?

9. What are some biblical examples of Jesus showing concern for individual people?

10. How have you grown in your relationship with Jesus during this part of the study?

11. Name two or three specific ways you are trying to be different as a result of this study.

12. In what ways has this study affected your attitude toward others?

Self-Evaluation

Your group leader will be meeting with you to discuss your current spiritual condition and your hopes for growing in your faith. Please take some time to reflect honestly on where you stand right now within these four basic categories of Christian growth. Rate yourself in each category.

+ DOING WELL. I'M PLEASED WITH MY PROGRESS SO FAR.

x ON THE RIGHT TRACK, BUT I SEE DEFINITE AREAS FOR IMPROVEMENT.

− THIS IS A STRUGGLE. I NEED SOME HELP.

A Disciple Is One Who . . .

13. *Walks with God.* To what extent is my Bible study and prayer time adequate for helping me walk with God?

Rating: _____

Comments:

14. *Lives the Word.* To what extent is my mind filled with scriptural truths so that my actions and reactions show I am being transformed?

Rating: _____

Comments:

15. *Contributes to the work.* To what extent am I actively participating in the church with my time, talents, and treasures?

Rating: _____

Comments:

16. *Impacts the world.* To what extent am I impacting my world with a Christian witness and influence?

Rating: _____

Comments:

17. Other issues I would like to discuss with my small-group leader:

PART 3

FOLLOWING JESUS

The Bible describes salvation as a free gift. Yet Jesus also spoke of discipleship as costly and urged those who would follow him to count the cost (see Luke 14:26–33). For Jesus, no final conflict existed between receiving his gracious forgiveness and following his exacting lordship. He knew that as Savior he was offering something to sinful people that they couldn't earn, yet as their Lord he was calling them to a life of service that required obedience at every turn. The concept of receiving the gift without deference to the Giver was unthinkable.

To take part in the relationship ("Savior" and "Forgiver") without embracing *all* Jesus is ("Master" and "Leader") would be as ridiculous as going through a marriage ceremony without anticipating a lifetime of loving and serving your spouse. Technically, you don't become married just by acting like you're married, and you don't become a Christian by living a good life, but would it make any sense to become married with no intention of acting like it? Does it make sense to receive Christ without responding daily in obedience to his commands?

In Ephesians 2:8–9, Paul writes that it is God's unconditional grace that saves us. But in the next verse, he tells us that God prepared good works for us to do (see verse 10). In Part 3 of this study, "Following Jesus," we will examine in greater detail what it means to follow Christ as Lord, day by day. This will bring you and your group members to a point where you can identify areas for personal growth and what, in particular, you need to do to make the lordship of Christ more functional in your lives.

PROTECTION AND DIRECTION

PERSONAL STUDY: 1 Peter 1; Matthew 16

SCRIPTURE MEMORY: Luke 6:46; 1 Corinthians 10:31

ON YOUR OWN: Jesus' Promise to Be with Us in All Circumstances

"Anything under God's control is never out of control."

—CHARLES R. SWINDOLL

Follow Me . . . I'll Protect You

A small child was once asked to sit down in the car. "I can't drive until you sit and buckle your seat belt," the mother said.

"No," replied the child.

"I will tell you again—sit down and buckle your belt."

"No," was the defiant answer.

"You either sit down and obey me, or we'll both get out of the car and I'll spank you!" responded the exasperated mother.

The child just glared at her silently. As the mother began to open the car door to make good on her threat, the child immediately sat down and buckled the belt.

"That's better," the mother said.

As they began to drive off, the child said under his breath—but loud enough to be heard, "I may be sitting down on the outside, but I'm standing up on the inside."

This story illustrates several important concepts about obedience. First, obedience maintains interpersonal harmony, while its opposite—disobedience—causes conflicts. When someone disobeys an authority, friction occurs between the two. Second, when the person issuing directives does the right thing, the recipient's obedience is for their well-being. Third, obedience is not the same as mere conformity to someone else's wishes. How often are we "standing up on the inside" even though we're "sitting down on the outside"?

True obedience is done willingly out of our trust in the one with authority. Conformity is merely begrudging adjustment of our outward actions. In this study, we will explore what it means to obey Christ and look at some steps we can use to help us obey God in any area.

What Is Obedience?

1. What does it mean to have authority?

2. In what ways do you respond (or have you responded) to the authority of . . .

the government?

a parent?

a coach?

the church?

3. What does it mean in practical (rather than theological) terms to call Jesus "Lord" (see Luke 6:46)?

4. What does your level of obedience to God show you (see John 14:15)?

5. Who does Jesus say are his "brothers and sisters" in Matthew 12:47–50?

Why Is Obedience to God So Important?

6. What effect does your obedience have on God (see 1 Thessalonians 4:1–2)?

7. According to the following verses, in what ways does obedience protect you?

Psalm 32:3–7

Psalm 119:45

Romans 1:25–31

8. How has obedience to God protected you?

9. According to the following verses, what effect does obedience and disobedience have on your conscience?

Ephesians 4:18–19

1 Timothy 1:19

1 Timothy 4:2

10. According to the following verses, what different effects can obedience to God have on your relationships with others?

Luke 6:22–23

Luke 6:27–28

Follow Me . . . I'll Direct You

Imagine for a moment that lately your boss has been pressuring you to put in excessive overtime hours. You've been talking with him about Christ, and you feel a heightened responsibility to live rightly. You wonder, *Should I submit to my boss's pressure to work at this hectic pace?*

Your daughter, meanwhile, has been invited to the prom by a non-Christian guy. She is seventeen, and you want to give her the right amount of freedom without letting her make a poor decision. To what extent should you intervene as she decides whether to accept?

On the way home from work, you're reminded that your car is getting old and on the brink of falling apart. Sometime soon you will need to replace it. As a Christian, does it matter what kind of car you get or how much you spend on it?

Most of what you do in life is not regulated by specific commands of Scripture. You work, go to school, shop, and do many other activities that require you to use your judgment. So, how can you be sure of always making the right choices? What does it mean to obey Christ in the "gray" areas?

Questions for Evaluating Questions for Your Actions

11. A first question to ask is, *Is this activity beneficial in any way?* What are some examples of activities that may be permissible but not necessarily beneficial (see 1 Corinthians 6:12)?

12. What is something that is permissible to some but not beneficial for you?

13. A second question is, *Does the activity master me?* What are some activities that could master a person (see 1 Corinthians 6:12)?

14. What activities do you need to guard against becoming master over you?

15. A third question is, *Could this activity hurt someone else's walk with God?* Why should you limit your freedom (see 1 Corinthians 10:24)?

16. How could a neutral or permissible activity hurt someone else (see 1 Corinthians 8:13)?

17. A fourth question is, *Does this activity glorify God?* What does it mean to glorify God (see 1 Corinthians 10:31)?

18. How can everyday actions (like eating and drinking) bring glory to God?

Your Walk with God

Bible

Schedule three times this week to be alone with God. Each day, read the passage indicated below and answer the questions that follow.

DAY ONE: 1 PETER 1

Some of the things I observe in this passage:

One idea for how to apply this passage to my life:

DAY TWO: MATTHEW 16:1–12

Some of the things I observe in this passage:

One idea for how to apply this passage to my life:

DAY THREE: MATTHEW 16:13–28

Some of the things I observe in this passage:

One idea for how to apply this passage to my life:

Prayer

On each of your three days with God this week, pray for the following:

Day One (Adoration): Read Psalm 135 in an attitude of prayer. List ten ways God has shown his faithfulness to you.

Day Two (Confession): Identify a sin you struggle with regularly. Try to find a verse that speaks directly to that sin. Meditate on that verse.

Day Three (Thanksgiving): Give thanks to God for three qualities in your spouse or a close friend. Then tell that person about what you were thankful for. Also thank God for who he made you to be—physically, relationally, mentally, and emotionally. Be specific in your prayer.

Scripture Memory

Memorize these verses this week:

> *Why do you call me, "Lord, Lord," and do not do what I say?* (Luke 6:46).

> *So whether you eat or drink or whatever you do, do it all for the glory of God* (1 Corinthians 10:31).

Next week, we will explore what it means for Jesus to be Lord over who we are and what we have. To prepare, think about the possessions you would most hate to lose.

On Your Own: Jesus' Promise to Be with Us in All Circumstances

How can someone who is not physically with us protect us and guide us? Jesus promised to be with us always (see Matthew 28:20). What does that look like in our daily lives?

Although Jesus is no longer with us physically, many of the details of his life, actions, and teachings from the time he came to earth and lived among people are recorded in the Gospels. We have four different perspectives on his life, which together provide an excellent picture of who Jesus was and what he taught. When we read the Gospels, it is as if we are spending time with Jesus and learning from him.

Jesus' presence with us is even more substantial as we read the Bible and pray, asking him to help us. He will be faithful to do so, and the Holy Spirit will also illuminate Jesus' words and guide our thoughts. Here are some things to consider as we seek to have Jesus' protection and direction for our lives:

- *Obedience:* There are good reasons why Jesus' directions and commands can be trusted.
- *Authority:* Jesus' authority is different from worldly authority, and therefore, is reliable.
- *Protection:* Obedience to Jesus protects us from harm because his commands guard us from painful outcomes that we might otherwise not see or ignore.

Jesus said to his disciples—and, by extension, to us—that he considers us friends (see John 15:15). And Jesus is the best kind of friend: one who will tell us the truth and give us excellent advice, one who will have our best interests at heart but not just tell us what he thinks we want to hear.

Trust and Obey

Jesus did not give arbitrary commands or create rules for the sake of having rules. In fact, he often tried to simplify the life of faith. He summarized hundreds of Old Testament laws with just two commands: (1) love God with all you've got, and (2) love your neighbor.

Of course, *simple* does not necessarily mean *easy.* Jesus told us to love our enemies (see Matthew 5:44). He told us that calling people fools was just as bad as killing them (see Matthew 5:21–22), and that looking at someone with lust was equivalent to adultery (see Matthew 5:27–28). On our own, we might never be able to obey Jesus' commands. But when we trust him, he gives us the power to obey. He gives us power to love God and to love others.

Jesus said, "Walk with me and work with me—watch how I do it. Learn the unforced rhythms of grace" (Matthew 11:29 MSG). He never asked us to do more than he was willing to do himself. He said we should love our enemies—and then he forgave those who were executing him (see Luke 23:34). If for no other reason, we can trust Jesus' commands because he, the Son of God, lived by them every moment he was on earth.

Authority without Abuse

Many of us breathe prayers to God for help—especially when we mess up—and God is willing to be gracious to us in such times. However, if we had just made different choices in accordance with Jesus' teachings, many of these problems wouldn't have occurred in the first place. We want God's help, but we also need to be willing to yield to his authority. To not accept his authority is like wanting to stay dry when it's raining but refusing to stay under the umbrella. God's rightful authority over us is a big part of what protects us, and rejecting it subjects us to needless difficulties.

If people who are over us in our lives have abused their authority, it can be difficult for us to trust. Power is granted to leaders so they can protect their followers—not take advantage of them. The good news is that Jesus is a leader unlike any we've ever followed. He never abuses his authority. He always has our best interests in mind. His directions and commands protect us and provide for us. He does not give them so he can dominate us or as a means for us to get on his good side; his commands are the way for us to find a truly abundant life.

Jesus was God incarnate, with full authority, yet he was gentle and humble. He didn't force his way on anyone, and he never manipulated people. He knew there would be times when some would not accept his teachings, and though it broke his heart, he did not coerce them to stay (see, for example, Mark 10:17–27 and John 6:60–69). That's the kind of leader we would all like to follow.

Protection and Presence

Jesus protects us, but that does not mean we won't have struggles or trials in our lives. Rather, he will be with us during those difficult times.

If we live according to the way of Jesus, and we behave in generous, loving, and respectful ways, those behaviors will partially protect us from harm. We'll have healthy, loving relationships and be known as peacemakers, not troublemakers. Within the loving boundaries Jesus sets for his followers, we can experience both protection and his presence.

God hears our prayers for protection and responds in love. "Keep me safe, my God, for in you I take refuge. I say to the LORD, 'You are my Lord; apart from you I have no good thing. . . . LORD, you alone are my portion and my cup; you make my lot secure. The boundary lines have fallen for me in pleasant places; surely I have a delightful inheritance'" (Psalm 16:1–2, 5–6). We can make that prayer from the Bible our prayer and be confident God will answer it.

JESUS THE LORD

PERSONAL STUDY: Matthew 19–21
SCRIPTURE MEMORY: Matthew 16:24;
1 Corinthians 9:25
ON YOUR OWN: A Word about Finances

"Thou hast made us for thyself, O Lord, and our heart is restless until it finds its rest in thee."
—AUGUSTINE OF HIPPO, *CONFESSIONS*

Lord of Who We Are

In the hearts of countless Americans, few events are more fascinating than a romance between celebrities. The media eagerly snatches up every detail of the courtship and reports them to a fascinated public. The couple makes orchestrated public appearances, exuding radiant smiles and tender looks for each other as the photographers take picture after picture. Finally, they announce wedding plans, vowing their relationship will last forever. The ceremony is a lavish spectacle, attended by admiring peers and surrounded by fans who hope to catch a glimpse of their idols. Yes, this must be love . . . or is it?

Soon, disturbing stories emerge of discord between the couple. They are seen less frequently together, and soon it becomes evident that the fairy-tale romance has lost its magic. Rumors circulate that both partners are seeing other people. Within a year, the stories are borne out by an announcement of a pending divorce. Recriminations fly between the couple in the media, and reporters find fresh copy, digging up the details about new relationships each partner has begun.

Why do so many romances among the famous (and not-so-famous) end in disaster? One obvious answer might be that people fail to perceive the commitment necessary to maintain a relationship. It is easy to take that first step and pledge lifelong devotion to another person. Yet when problems and conflicts happen, it requires self-sacrifice and hard work to make those commitments stick.

Your life as a Christian requires that same kind of devotion if you are to remain an effective servant for God. In this study, you will gain an understanding of what it means to be a disciple of the *Lord* Jesus Christ, submitting to his lordship (especially as it relates to handling your resources), and the benefits for doing so.

Denying Self

1. The key verse for this study is Matthew 16:24, where Jesus said to his disciples, "Whoever wants to be my disciple must deny themselves and take up their cross and follow me." If you were with the disciples when Jesus said this, how might you have reacted?

2. What does it mean to "deny yourself"? What should you deny or say no to?

3. In what area has it been hard for you to deny yourself lately?

Take Up Your Cross

4. What did it mean for a person to literally take up a cross in Jesus' day?

5. What truth about walking with God was Jesus trying to communicate when he said "take up [your] cross"?

6. Why is it uncomfortable or unnatural to take up your cross?

7. Why is it important to take up your cross daily?

Follow Christ

8. What are some other words that mean the same as *follow*?

9. In what ways do you find it easy to imitate Jesus? In what ways is it difficult to imitate Jesus?

10. In what area of life do you want to become more like Jesus? How will you
    do this?

Lord of What We Have

The rich young man had no money problems. His every material need was easily met, and he had power, comfort, and prestige. Yet something inside him sensed that he still needed something to be truly satisfied. So he came to Jesus hoping for affirmation and comfort.

But when Jesus exposed the source of the young ruler's restlessness, he balked. He probably could have made any other sacrifice, but being required to surrender his wealth was too threatening, for it was the foundation of his security. His money problem was not a lack of means but rather an excessive dependence on it.

Christians sometimes have the same struggles as the rich young man. Reliance on wealth can create bondage and anxiety for believers as well as for nonbelievers. But a big part of being Christ's disciple is handling your resources in a way that honors God. That's a tough challenge, but you can meet it.

The Rich Young Man

11. *Read Matthew 19:16–30.* What details do we know about this man who came
    to see Jesus (see Matthew 19:22)?

12. What did Jesus accomplish by his response to the young man's question (see
    Matthew 19:17)?

13. According to Jesus, what was the man's problem (see Matthew 19:21)?

14. Why did Jesus say that it is hard for rich people to enter the kingdom of heaven (see Matthew 19:23–24)?

15. What do you most want to remember about Jesus' talk with the rich young man?

Lord of All

Have you ever signed up for a "free offer," only to find out you were going to be billed $19.95 for it? Perhaps you were one of the lucky winners of a "free gift," only to find out you had to listen to a two-hour sales pitch to claim it. "There's no such thing as a free lunch," as the saying goes. You pay a price for almost everything.

This is as true of following Christ as it is in any other area of life. The costs of being a disciple of Christ involve (1) denying yourself, (2) taking up your cross, (3) following Christ, and (4) submitting all you have to the Lord. It is not hard to see from this list that the cost is substantial. But the cost is one worth paying. Jesus didn't hold back from telling his disciples of the benefits of following him.

The Costs

16. What are the costs of following Christ?

17. What did you have to give up to become a Christian?

Some of the Benefits of Following Christ

- *God's provision* (see Matthew 6:33)
- *Freedom* (see John 8:32)
- *Peace of mind* (see John 14:27)
- *Joy* (see John 15:11)
- *Peace with God* (see Romans 5:1–2)
- *God's love* (see Romans 5:5–8)
- *Hope of heaven* (see Romans 5:9–10)
- *Character development* (see Romans 8:28–29)
- *Access to God* (see Hebrews 4:16)

18. Which two or three of the above benefits are the most important to you? Why?

Apply It to Your Life

19. Why is it worth paying the price to follow Christ (see 1 Corinthians 9:24–27)?

Your Walk with God

Bible

Schedule three times this week to be alone with God. Each day, read the passage indicated below and answer the questions that follow.

DAY ONE: MATTHEW 19

Some of the things I observe in this passage:

One idea for how to apply this passage to my life:

DAY TWO: MATTHEW 20

Some of the things I observe in this passage:

One idea for how to apply this passage to my life:

Day Three: Matthew 21

In what way were these events "the beginning of the end" for Jesus?

One idea for how to apply this passage to my life:

Prayer

On each of your three days with God this week, pray for the following:

Day One (Adoration): Paraphrase Psalm 139:1–18 as a prayer of adoration to God and pray through it.

Day Two (Confession): Let the Holy Spirit convict you and list two or three sins you would especially like to defeat in your life. Ask God to replace these with characteristics of his.

Day Three (Thanksgiving): Thank God for one thing or person you've taken for granted lately.

Scripture Memory

Memorize these verses this week:

Then Jesus said to his disciples, "Whoever wants to be my disciple must deny themselves and take up their cross and follow me" (Matthew 16:24).

Everyone who competes in the games goes into strict training. They do it to get a crown that will not last, but we do it to get a crown that will last forever (1 Corinthians 9:25).

In the next study, we will take a closer look at the expectations we have for God and the opposition Jesus experienced during his ministry. To prepare, consider whether you expect God to give you a life free from difficulty. Do you sometimes find yourself thinking that God owes you something? When has following Christ produced negative reactions in others? How did you respond? What problems or opportunities did this create for you?

On Your Own: A Word about Finances

The Bible has more to say about money than just about any other subject. Maybe that's because money holds the potential for great kingdom gain—or great personal loss. Marriages break up over it, careers are shaped by it, needs are supplied through it, and lives are shipwrecked if it is mismanaged.

An integral part of being a disciple of Jesus Christ is handling our resources in a God-honoring way. In our culture, that poses a tough challenge. Some of us may be like the rich young man, and we do not yet recognize our obeisance and obedience to another god. Or we may tend to the opposite extreme: we are always longing for money but never have it. We may worship the same god as the rich young man—only we do so from a distance. Many of us will be somewhere in the middle. Whatever our situation, it is important to note that *proper money management—stewardship—is essential for a mature follower of Jesus Christ.*

Included below is a statement written by elders at Willow Creek Community Church that outlines some guidelines for giving as a Christian. Although this represents just one church's wrestling with the issue, it provides wise counsel for anyone seeking to understand the place of finances in the life of a Christian.

■ ■ ■

In Old Testament times, God's people were required to contribute at least a tenth of their income to God's work (the tithe). Although the New Testament is not explicit about the continued validity of the standard, it may be assumed that it endorses the practice of tithing as a minimum guideline or a starting point for

Christian giving. The New Testament lays demands upon believers that exceed the giving of the tithe.

According to the New Testament, the totality of one's possessions belongs to God—not just the tithe (see Matthew 6:19–34; 19:16–30; 25:14–30; Luke 9:23–25; 12:13–34; 16:1–13; 18:18–30; 21:1–4; Acts 2:44–45; 4:32–37; 1 Timothy 6:6–10).

The New Testament allows Christians to keep the portion of their income necessary to provide for themselves and their dependents so they do not become a burden on society (see 1 Thessalonians 4:11–12; 1 Timothy 5:8). But the balance of their income is to be used for God's work and for deeds of charity (see 2 Corinthians 9:6–15; Galatians 6:10; 1 Timothy 6:17–19; James 2:15–16; 1 John 3:16–18).

Thus, whereas the Old Testament required the contribution of only a tenth of one's income to God's work, the New Testament requires the total disposition of one's possessions for God's work, except for that portion which is to be kept to provide for oneself and one's relatives with reasonable safeguards for the future. On this basis, if a tenth of one's income is sufficient to provide for one's own and family needs, the remaining 90 percent belongs to God's work.

This approach to giving reflects the radical transformation of worldly, materialistic values that takes place under the impact of the gospel, as the quest for personal advantage gives way to the desire to worship God through total disposition of oneself to his service and to the service of others (see Romans 12:1).

The expansion of the old covenant standard of tithing into the principle of total giving provides an explanation for the relative silence on this issue of tithing in the New Testament. The implications of the New Testament principle of total disposition reduce tithing to a beginner's exercise, a minimum reference that is to be increased in proportion to one's income and one's growth in Christ.

For Christians whose limited income is only sufficient for subsistence, the tithe provides a goal to attain. For more affluent Christians whose income exceeds their needs, the tithe becomes restrictive. It is to be surpassed in the same measure that God prospers them.

To ensure the proper functioning of the ministries of the local church, it is appropriate for a body of believers to expect that, apart from other giving, at least one tenth of their constituents' income will be contributed to the local church that serves them. Both the Old and New Testaments offer warrant upholding such a standard (see Leviticus 27:30–32; Malachi 3:10; Matthew 23:23). The New Testament enjoins believers to support generously the ministry of their local church (see 1 Corinthians 9:11–14; Galatians 6:6).

According to the New Testament, the responsibility for the proper apportionment of a believer's giving is a matter of individual conscience rather than a function of the body. However, the church is to exercise watchcare over its constituency to protect it from the sin of greed, which is cause for church discipline and excommunication (see 1 Corinthians 5:10–11; Ephesians 5:3; Colossians 3:5).

When Christians learn to regard the totality of "their" possessions as belonging not to themselves but to God, they develop a joyful sense of freedom from the instinct of possessiveness. They view their possessions as divine entrustments placed in their care for the purpose of ministry. As a result, their giving is not based on legalistic calculations of grudgingly accepted impositions. It becomes the spontaneous heart response of grateful spirits answering cheerfully and generously to God's love. The biblical measure for giving is to be found in a grateful heart, not in the devices of an electronic calculator (see Acts 20:35).

JESUS UNDER ATTACK

PERSONAL STUDY: Matthew 22–24
SCRIPTURE MEMORY: Luke 6:22
ON YOUR OWN: Jesus in Jerusalem

"For you will certainly carry out God's purpose, however you act, but it makes a difference to you whether you serve like Judas or like John."
—C. S. LEWIS, *THE PROBLEM OF PAIN*

The Beginning of the End

Expectations have a way of setting you up for disappointment. Consider, for example, some of the actions you expect from your family or friends—perhaps keeping you informed of their whereabouts or taking out the trash every Thursday night. Whether these expectations are realistic doesn't matter; you have come to depend on them. What happens when they aren't met?

Palm Sunday was a clash of expectations. Jesus had arrived in Jerusalem six days before the Passover, one of the most important holidays in the Jewish calendar. Thousands of people had crammed into Jerusalem to observe the feast. Shortly before he entered the city, he had raised Lazarus from the dead. When people heard about it, the anticipation built for what he would do next.

Many people fully expected Jesus to liberate them from Rome. He was greeted by a throng of admiring locals. But those expectations did not match Jesus' mission. Rather than coming to conquer Rome, he had come to conquer sin; his aims were spiritual, not political. Some sort of letdown was inevitable. And so, when it became clear that Jesus would not use his power for nationalistic ends, his popularity plummeted—so much so that the crowds who cheered for him at the beginning of the week were easily coaxed into calling for his crucifixion only a few days later. Festive Palm Sunday was, ironically, the beginning of the end for Jesus.

In this study, we will focus on Palm Sunday, one of the key events in God's unfolding plan of salvation, and see how the religious leaders in Jerusalem attempted to trap Jesus. We will also learn how to handle opposition by seeing the way Jesus responded.

The Triumphal Entry

1. How did the crowds greet Jesus as he was riding into the city of Jerusalem (see Matthew 21:1–11)?

2. Why did the crowds gather to greet Jesus (see John 12:9–11, 17–18)?

3. What is the significance of Jesus riding in on a donkey (see Zechariah 9:9)?

4. Why did the crowds say what they did about Jesus (see Matthew 21:9–11)?

The Rejection

5. Nearly a week later, after Jesus had been arrested and tried, the crowd condemned Jesus to die (see Matthew 27:15–26). How could the crowd reject Jesus so soon after they had hailed him as their king?

6. We sometimes want God to act in ways that compromise his character. What are some examples of expecting what we shouldn't from God?

7. When was a time that you expected God to act a certain way and he refused?

8. In what ways do you need to adjust your expectations of God at this point in your life?

9. How should you adjust your expectations in order to serve God totally (see John 12:24–26)?

10. In what ways do you imagine God wants you to focus less on you using him and more on allowing him to use you for his purposes?

11. When has God used a painful event in your life to accomplish something good in or through you?

The Trap

Most people want to be liked by somebody—to feel affirmed, appreciated, and important. Who hasn't done something with the hope that "so-and-so will really be pleased"? Whether it be your parents, your boss, the crowd, or a personal mentor, the desire to please can be a great motivator.

But being liked was not at the top of Jesus' priorities. Rather, he did what was *right*—what the Father wanted him to do—despite the costs; and he taught others that they should do the same. His healings did gain him many admirers, but he did not heal people to win their favor or seek their recognition. While the crowds liked him, his hard stand against hypocrisy exposed the religious leaders of his day, and over time he gained more and more enemies. While Jesus knew this, he never altered his deeds or words to halt the defection.

Christians who live their faith openly will encounter opposition just as Jesus did. For that reason, we should do all we can to prepare for it.

Jesus Under Attack

12. How did the religious leaders try to trap Jesus (see Matthew 21:23–27; 22:15–46)?

13. Why did the Pharisees and others try to trap Jesus (see Matthew 22:15–46)?

Jesus' Response

14. For what did Jesus condemn the religious leaders (see Matthew 23:1–39)?

15. What can you learn from the Pharisees' negative example?

Apply It to Your Life

16. What sort of opposition does Jesus receive today?

17. What can you learn from the way Jesus responded to opposition?

18. When was a time in the past when you experienced opposition for being a Christian?

19. Why might experiencing opposition be a sign of obedience to God (see 2 Timothy 3:12)?

20. In what ways can Christians bring unnecessary criticism and opposition on themselves (mistakenly thinking they are "following Jesus" with such words or actions)?

Your Walk with God

Bible

Schedule three times this week to be alone with God. Each day, read the passage indicated below and answer the questions that follow.

DAY ONE: MATTHEW 22

Some of the things I observe in this passage:

One idea for how to apply this passage to my life:

DAY TWO: MATTHEW 23

Some of the things I observe in this passage:

One idea for how to apply this passage to my life:

DAY THREE: MATTHEW 24

Some of the things I observe in this passage:

One idea for how to apply this passage to my life:

Prayer

This week, it's your turn to come up with creative prayer ideas. Use the basic ACTS format, but identify your own specific emphases. Be prepared next week to share what you did for each.

Adoration:	
Confession:	
Thanksgiving:	
Supplication:	

Scripture Memory

Memorize this verse this week:

> *"Blessed are you when people hate you, when they exclude you and insult*
> *you and reject your name as evil, because of the Son of Man"* (Luke 6:22).

In the next study, we will learn about Christ's promise to return. To prepare, consider what emotions that event evokes in you.

On Your Own: Jesus in Jerusalem

As Jesus set his face like a flint toward Jerusalem (see Luke 9:51), he was heading into a well-planned trap. We may wonder why he would do that. The trap was so obvious to almost everyone, yet he went anyway.

Jesus was not oblivious to what was happening. As he led the parade into Jerusalem on Palm Sunday, he was not fooled by the cheering crowds. He knew that he would soon be rejected by the very ones who applauded him. The unbroken donkey colt that he rode in on was a fulfillment of prophecy (see Zechariah 9:9), which most of the adoring crowd, mistaking Jesus for a political messiah, misunderstood. He rode on a beast of burden, not a triumphant warhorse. It was just one of many signals Jesus was sending that his mission was different than what most people expected.

It's easy to capitulate to people's demands when their expectations are high. Jesus, however, did not. He stayed focused, even when his agenda didn't seem to make sense to the people around him. He focused on God's will, God's strength, and God's plan for redemption through suffering rather than letting well-meaning friends pull him off track (see, for example, Matthew 16:21–23).

In this pivotal time in his life, Jesus handled attack with both humility and strength. He set firm boundaries but didn't run away from the hardships that were before him. Our challenge is to do the same.

Clarity of Calling

Jesus knew that he had come to earth ultimately to die, and as his followers, we are called to "take up [our] cross" as well (see Matthew 16:24). Most of us will not be called to physical martyrdom, but we must be ready to set aside our own preferences so we can serve others. We must learn to love not just when we feel like it but also when it is hard. We must, at times, sacrifice our comfort so others' needs can be met.

Beyond that, God has a specific calling for each of us that fits our gifts and wiring. Some of us are called to teach, or lead, or write, or build a church, or serve the poor, or comfort those who are sick or dying. Jesus was clear on his calling, and he didn't let other people pull him in directions that may have been good but weren't what his Father wanted for him. Following his example means taking time to earnestly pray about God's will and his mission for our lives. We cannot do everything, and we certainly cannot meet everybody else's expectations, so we must bravely answer the call God has for us even if it is difficult or not everybody understands.

So often, well-meaning friends or family try to control us or tell us how they think we ought to live. Like Jesus, we have to set firm boundaries. In John 7:1–13, we read one story of how Jesus' brothers tried to manage his "career" by telling him what to do. Jesus rejected their advice because he knew the path he had to travel.

While we are called to love our family, this does not mean we let them control us. Jesus showed us that we don't have to be "people pleasers," but should gently and firmly set boundaries. When someone says, "You need to do this," we should be wise and discerning. Those people may be trying to advance their own agenda—a good thing, but not necessarily *our* thing. Or perhaps, like Jesus' brothers, they might be skeptical of our calling and behave in a passive-aggressive way. Neither reason is sufficient to take us off the path God lays out for us.

Empowered by Prayer

Jesus stayed focused on his mission, even as his friends betrayed him and abandoned him. Although he was unjustly accused, sentenced, and led off to execution, he did not exert his power to get out of his responsibility. Certainly, the ability to stay strong was a function of his being the Son of God; yet the night before his death, he spent a long time praying. That too contributed to his endurance, and he calls us to pray for strength as well.

When you find yourself in difficult situations, follow Jesus to the garden of Gethsemane and pray (see Matthew 26:36–46; Luke 22:39–46). Ask God to help you stay on track and resist attack. Pray courageously as Jesus did, "Not my will but yours be done." And remember that while you may find yourself under attack, you can always trust in Jesus. The ultimate victory belongs to him. Because you are his, it belongs to you as well.

READY FOR HIS RETURN

PERSONAL STUDY: Matthew 25–26
SCRIPTURE MEMORY: Matthew 16:25
ON YOUR OWN: Jesus' Promise to Come Back

"We are to wait for the coming of Christ with patience. We are to watch with anticipation. We are to work with zeal. We are to prepare with urgency."

—BILLY GRAHAM

Living in Light of Jesus' Return

We are always getting ready for something. We get ready for bed, for work, for dinner, for retirement. We prepare meals and prepare for dinner guests. The more important the upcoming event, the more time and energy we spend preparing for it.

Jesus has not finished what he set out to do among us. When Jesus ascended into heaven, he didn't leave this earth permanently. When all other great religious leaders died, they left behind their teachings, their example, their followers, and their corpses. Only Jesus rose—bodily—from the dead. And only Jesus will return—bodily—to earth.

When Jesus does return, he will bring about the culmination of history as we know it. He will answer all our questions. He will assume his final place as Lord, as every knee bows. He will expose and judge all evil deeds. And he will fulfill all of God's promises.

Following Jesus means living in the light of that truth. Not only is our Savior alive, and not only is he with us through the Holy Spirit, but he is also coming again!

Be on the Alert for His Coming

1. *Read Matthew* 24:26–35. What do you observe about the second coming of Christ?

2. In what ways can you ready yourself for Christ's coming?

3. How can you remind yourself that Jesus will return?

4. What distracts you from being "on the alert"?

The Two Kinds of Servants

5. *Read Matthew 24:45–51.* What do the main characters in this parable represent?

6. What does Jesus say the faithful and wise servant does (see Matthew 24:45–46)?

7. What reward does this servant receive (see Matthew 24:47)?

8. What does Jesus say the wicked servant does (see Matthew 24:48–49)?

9. What loss does this servant experience (see Matthew 24:50–51)?

10. In what ways have you been like each of these slaves?

The Ten Virgins

11. *Read Matthew 25:1–13.* Who are the main characters in this parable?

12. What did the foolish virgins do? What did the wise virgins do (see Matthew 25:2–4)?

13. What happened to each group when the bridegroom arrived (see Matthew 25:7–10)?

14. How does this parable challenge you?

The Talents

15. *Read Matthew 25:14–30.* Who are the main characters in this parable?

16. Why did the master call the first two servants "good and faithful" (see Matthew 25:21, 23)?

17. Why did the master call the third servant wicked and lazy (see Matthew 25:26)?

18. Where do you need to be more faithful with what God has given to you?

Apply It to Your Life

19. What simple step or activity could you do this week that would help you be more prepared for Christ's coming?

Your Walk with God

Bible

Schedule three times this week to be alone with God. Each day, read the passage indicated below and answer the questions that follow.

DAY ONE: MATTHEW 25:1–30

Some of the things I observe in this passage:

One idea for how to apply this passage to my life:

DAY TWO: MATTHEW 25:31–26:16

Some of the things I observe in this passage:

One idea for how to apply this passage to my life:

DAY THREE: MATTHEW 26:17–75

Some of the things I observe in this passage:

One idea for how to apply this passage to my life:

Prayer

On each of your three days with God this week, pray for the following:

Day One (Adoration): During the events described in Matthew 26, right before Jesus died on the cross, he said no to many natural human desires. What were those desires? What other godly attributes did he display in resisting those temptations?

Day Two (Confession): To what selfish desires do you need to die in order to live for God?

Day Three (Supplication): Pray for God to help you die to the desires you listed.

Scripture Memory

Memorize this verse this week:

"For whoever wants to save their life will lose it, but whoever loses their life for me will find it" (Matthew 16:25).

The next study is about Jesus being betrayed, his commitment to doing the Father's will, his crucifixion, and his death. To prepare for the study, consider what about God's will you struggle with. What does it mean to pray to God, "Your will be done"?

On Your Own: Jesus' Promise to Come Back

Jesus often used terms of investment and economics in his illustrations about the kingdom of God. For example, he compared the kingdom of God to a buried treasure or a valuable pearl (see Matthew 13:44–46).

He also used an economic metaphor to talk about his return to earth. His story of three servants, each of whom were entrusted with "talents" (meaning *bags of gold*) to invest, is sobering. The master in the story rewarded the servants who invested and got him a good return. He chastised the servant who simply buried his treasure in the ground (see Matthew 25:14–30).

This parable, sandwiched between two others with similar themes of preparation and consequences, raises the questions: *With what has God entrusted you that he will expect you to use in his service? What has he given to you to invest and grow for him?*

We could take the parable quite literally. We have financial resources, which we can invest for God's purposes and bring about a return. The benefits of those investments are not for ourselves, but for our master. But the parable is also understood to communicate the importance of using our *spiritual* gifts—our talents in the sense of abilities—to further the work of God. We must not bury our gifts, but rather use and develop them to build God's kingdom.

Getting a Return

But how do we do that? What does a "good return" on the investment of our talents look like? We each must ask, *What "bag of gold" has God given to me?* Perhaps it is a skill—business acumen, for example—that brings financial returns. Maybe we can invest—literally—so as to make money that will help fund God's work. Or perhaps it is leadership, or a strong sense of being able to show mercy, or being ready with empowering encouragement. We all have differing abilities that God can use to spread his message, show his love, and build the church.

The parable in Matthew 25:31–46 provides specific ways that we can invest our time, money, and talents in God's kingdom. In this parable, Jesus spells out what it means to love as he loved: we must feed the hungry, clothe the naked, and visit the sick. So you must ask, *What gifts have I been given that God is asking me to invest?*

The Bible tells us that every believer has been given at least one spiritual gift—a divine enablement to do something that will further God's kingdom and build up the body of Christ (see 1 Corinthians 12, especially verse 7). Jesus seems to expect that each of us will take whatever skills or resources he has placed in us and use them to serve others. But in his parable, he doesn't say the master wanted his servants to spend the money on helping people. Instead, he wanted a *return* on it. How do we get a return on spiritual investments?

While we all have spiritual gifts, we can either choose to develop and hone those gifts or we can ignore them. Jesus invites us to do the former. Just imagine someone had the musical gift of perfect pitch—an amazing talent that musicians covet. To develop that gift, the person would need to actually sing and play instruments. He or she would have to learn and practice to use that gift to its fullest potential.

If that person did nothing with that ability, what good would it be to have perfect pitch? The gift would be wasted. Or if the person used it occasionally but never practiced, he or she might make some music but would never get better. Either way, the person would not be investing that skill to increase its return.

Whether you have a gift of leadership or teaching or mercy or helping, God invites you to take that gift and fully develop it. You can read about it, look for opportunities to use it (even with a small group of people), or put yourself in situations where you stretch yourself beyond your comfort zone. When you "practice" using your gifts, you get better at them, and the body of Christ (and the whole world, really) is blessed.

Prepared for His Return

When we are focused on developing and deploying our talents, we're aligned with what God is doing right now—and we are preparing for Jesus' return. The kingdom is both a current reality and something to look forward to. When we serve others using our resources and gifts, we invite them to be a part of God's kingdom now. In ways that aren't completely clear, we are also getting our world ready for his return (see 2 Peter 3:11–13).

Jesus soberly warns that he will "settle accounts" when he returns. He'll bless us for doing what he asked us to do: caring for the poor, the hungry, the sick, and the prisoner. That's an exciting prospect, and it can encourage us when the going gets tough.

Joy, fulfillment, and purpose are available now if we simply invest our talents for the kingdom. Will such a commitment be challenging? Of course it will! But it will be worth it. Jesus said whoever wants to gain their life must lose it (see Matthew 16:25). When we give, it comes back to us many times and beyond measure. Someday, we'll be able to share in our Master's happiness. And that joy can begin right now as we place our gifts and lives at his disposal.

THE CRUCIFIXION

PERSONAL STUDY: Matthew 27–28
SCRIPTURE MEMORY: Matthew 26:39; Romans 5:8
ON YOUR OWN: The Mystery of Pain and Suffering

*"But God is up in heaven and he doesn't do a thing,
with a million angels watching and they never move a
   wing.
It's God they ought to crucify instead of you and me,
said to this carpenter a-hanging on the tree."*
—SYDNEY CARTER

Betrayed!

Life is hard. Along with its joys and rewards come difficulties and disappointments. And getting older often means taking on more of life's burdens, not fewer of them. "What a heavy burden God has laid on mankind!" (Ecclesiastes 1:13).

Jesus' life was no different. In fact, his very mission was to suffer and die—unjustly. The price he paid—experiencing the crushing weight of our sin on the cross along with the physical anguish—cost him more than we can imagine. His suffering was intense not just while he was on the cross but even before, in the garden of Gethsemane when he faced the certainty of the pain he would suffer.

Yet Jesus willingly went through with his mission. Why? Because he wanted to do his Father's will more than anything else. His agonizing words, "Not as I will, but as you will" (Matthew 26:39), was not just a prayer. It was his life and mission.

This study will take you through the final preparations by Judas and the chief priests to arrest Jesus, and it will climax at the point in Jesus' trial where Peter denies him. It is a dismal chapter in the Gospels—but, as such, it is full of important warnings. No one can ever safely consider himself or herself bulletproof against the attacks of Satan. Rather, our prayer to God must perpetually be, "Not as I will, but as you will."

Jesus' Final Hours

1. *The plot to kill Jesus.* Why did the Jewish religious leaders plot to kill Jesus (see Matthew 26:1–5)? In what way is Jesus' lordship a threat to your authority over yourself?

2. *The costly perfume controversy.* Why did Jesus defend the woman for pouring expensive perfume on him (see Matthew 26:6–13)? Why is it important to be open to what God wants instead of only to your own view of what is practical or good?

3. *Judas arranges to betray Jesus.* How did Jesus' opponents get their opportunity to arrest Jesus (see Matthew 26:14–16)?

4. *The Last Supper.* What was the significance of Jesus' Last Supper with the disciples (see Matthew 26:17–30; John 13:1–17)? Why should you remember Jesus' Last Supper?

5. *The garden of Gethsemane.* What do you notice about Jesus and his disciples in the garden of Gethsemane (see Matthew 26:31–46)? What does this incident teach you about prayer and God's will?

6. *The betrayal and arrest of Jesus.* How was Jesus arrested (see Matthew 26:47–56)? What does it mean to betray or desert Jesus with our words or actions now?

7. *Jesus' trial before Caiaphas.* What is noteworthy about Jesus' trial before the high priest (see Matthew 26:57–68)? When is it better to say nothing than to defend yourself?

8. *Peter's denial.* What human tendencies do you see in Peter's denial of Christ (see Matthew 26:69–75)? How do believers today deny Christ, whether they realize it or not?

Jesus' Death and Burial

Christ's death is one of the most important topics we can study as Christians. More than just a painful death, the crucifixion was Christ's act of paying for *our* sins. He was mocked, humiliated, and rejected in paying for *our* guilt. It is easy to think of Christ's death only as an event that happened in the past. But if it weren't for Christ's death, our lives today would not be what they are.

As you read the story of Christ's death, imagine the scenes in your mind. See the soldiers' dirty faces, hear their sarcastic taunts, feel the marketplace heat, and imagine the thorns digging into Jesus' head. Try to imagine what it must have been like for Jesus to go through the suffering he faced. Put yourself right next to it all.

Jesus' Public Humiliation

9. What do you remember as one of your most painful experiences of rejection?

10. What are some of the specific sufferings that Jesus endured at his public trial (see Matthew 27:11–26)?

11. How did the soldiers cause Jesus to suffer (see Matthew 27:27–31)?

12. What emotions do these scenes evoke in you?

Jesus' Suffering on the Cross

13. What sufferings did Jesus endure on the cross (see Matthew 27:35–50)?

14. What emotions does this scene evoke in you?

15. What was most significant to you about Jesus' death on the cross?

16. What events happened right after the crucifixion (see Matthew 27:51–66)?

Apply It to Your Life

17. In summary, what have you learned about Jesus' commitment to the Father's will?

18. What have you learned about your own commitment to God's will?

Your Walk with God

Bible

Schedule three times this week to be alone with God. Each day, read the passage indicated below and answer the questions that follow.

DAY ONE: MATTHEW 27:1–26

Some of the things I observe in this passage:

One idea for how to apply this passage to my life:

DAY TWO: MATTHEW 27:27–66

Some of the things I observe in this passage:

One idea for how to apply this passage to my life:

DAY THREE: MATTHEW 28

Some of the things I observe in this passage:

One idea for how to apply this passage to my life:

Prayer

On each of your three days with God this week, pray for the following:

Day One (Adoration): Write a prayer in answer to the question, *What if Jesus had not been raised from the dead?* For example: "Father, if Jesus had not been raised from the dead, I _____ and you _____." Or: "Lord, I worship you for the resurrection of Jesus, because otherwise _____."

Day Two (Confession): Take a look back over the past month of your life. List the sins you remember being guilty of committing. List the acts of obedience you have been guilty of *not* doing. Confess these to God.

Day Three (Thanksgiving): Go over your list of confessions and write "paid in full" next to every sin. Thank God for forgiving each and every sin and for accepting you through his grace.

Scripture Memory

Memorize these verses this week:

> *Going a little farther, he fell with his face to the ground and prayed, "My Father, if it is possible, may this cup be taken from me. Yet not as I will, but as you will"* (Matthew 26:39).

> *But God demonstrates his own love for us in this: While we were still sinners, Christ died for us* (Romans 5:8).

Our next study will focus on the resurrection and Jesus' final words to his followers—known as the Great Commission. To prepare, consider why the resurrection is absolutely central to Christianity and how our Easter celebrations highlight or miss this important event. Also consider what Jesus wanted to impress on his disciples at the end of his ministry on earth.

On Your Own: The Mystery of Pain and Suffering

We've all been through times when life didn't seem to make sense. It's bewildering when pain or suffering hits us, or when our prayers seem to go unanswered, or when friends betray us or abandon us.

Jesus experienced these same trials. During his final hours, he was unfairly accused, misunderstood, betrayed, and ultimately killed. His prayer for relief—that the Father would "take this cup" from him—was answered with a resounding "no." His friends abandoned him, even though they had promised to be loyal. He was left completely alone, facing trumped-up charges, a breach of justice, torture, and death.

Jesus' suffering can help us by demonstrating how to surrender to God's will even if it means facing pain and struggle. God does not ask us to endure more than Christ did, and he offers comfort that he will be with us in the pain. Beyond that, he invites us to see there is always a greater purpose in our suffering.

Not My Will

Jesus wasn't just mouthing words when he asked God to take the cup of suffering from him—it was horrible to anticipate and even worse to live through. Yet he didn't end his prayer by stating his desire; rather, he yielded his will to his Father.

Where are you being asked to surrender your desire to God's greater good? What situation are you facing where it is hard to pray, "Not my will, but yours be done"? That is the very place where God is forming you spiritually, strengthening your character and inviting you into greater Christlikeness.

Surrendering to God's will may feel scary, but it is really a surrender to love. Even in life-and-death situations, God has our best interests at heart—just as he did for Jesus. Death is never the end of the story. Suffering is never our ultimate fate, though it may be present for a season.

When we surrender to God's purposes, it ultimately leads to joy. We have hope *in spite of* our circumstances, rather than hoping *in* our circumstances. Our faith grows when we pray "not my will" because what we get instead is "his will"—and his will is good.

Not Alone

In Jesus' betrayal, trial, and crucifixion we realize that he fully understands our pain. He isn't just sympathetic to our difficulties; he has experienced them himself. He asks us to die to self. But he's "taken his own medicine" and not asked us to do anything he himself has not done.

Christianity is not a spectator sport, but one in which we are invited to fully participate—for better or worse. Jesus predicted that we'd have troubles. But in the next breath, he promised that we would not be alone in those troubles—he would be with us always (see John 16:33; Matthew 28:20).

Jesus knows what it's like to feel lonely and experience pain. When a good friend has been through the same things you have, you know that he or she understands. Somehow, that's comforting, even though it's still hard. Jesus is our friend, and his suffering enables us to experience his love more deeply. We know that even as we choose to die to self, we are never alone.

Not Meaningless

One key to holding up in hard times is to recognize the larger purpose at work. Jesus' death was not meaningless, as horrible as it was. His death invites us to examine our own suffering from a different perspective. Facing our trials with faith (and even joy) develops our spiritual strength and maturity and helps us to build perseverance (see James 1:2–4).

What pain or struggle are we facing right now? What spiritual muscles is this difficulty helping us to develop? How does Christ's example encourage us and help us as we face it? When that pain feels pointless or meaningless, we can cry out to Jesus, who has also known pain and suffering. We can ask for wisdom and insight to help understand what brought this pain our way.

Sometimes, the pain is meant to correct or redirect us, because we've actually contributed to the hardship we're facing. Other times, the pain comes from circumstances we cannot control. We might actually be suffering for doing good—like refusing to cheat, lie, or compromise. In those times, we must entrust ourselves to God (see 1 Peter 4:19). Pain draws us closer to God. He may correct or comfort us, but he will always be with us.

Jesus could have wiggled out of his death sentence, but he knew the greater purpose of his suffering and death. When we keep our eyes on our purpose, our pain becomes a crucible in which our faith is purified and strengthened. That is not the whole answer to our suffering, but it is the one that matters most. And even when we don't know the purpose, we know the One who will someday show us why.

Until then, we have his love, comfort, and promise to get us through.

"For whatever reason God chose to make man as he is—limited and suffering and subject to sorrows and death—He had the honesty and courage to take His own medicine. Whatever game He is playing with His own creation, He has kept His own rules and played fair. He can exact nothing from man that He has not exacted from Himself."

—Dorothy Sayers

THE RESURRECTION

PERSONAL STUDY: Acts 1–2
SCRIPTURE MEMORY: 1 Corinthians 15:58
ON YOUR OWN: The Resurrection Story

"If Jesus rose from the dead, then you have to accept all that he said; if he didn't rise from the dead, then why worry about any of what he said? The issue on which everything hangs is not whether or not you like his teaching but whether or not he rose from the dead."
—TIMOTHY KELLER, *THE REASON FOR GOD*

A Pivotal Event

In our secular culture, Easter lives in the shadows of other holidays. Compared to Christmas, for example, Easter hardly makes an appearance. In most churches this is not the case, but for the vast majority of modern men and women, Easter comes and goes without much fanfare.

Yet Christ's resurrection is a pivotal event. It is absolutely central to the Christian faith. You could not be a Christian without it being true. Our salvation stands or falls with the resurrection of Jesus. Without the resurrection, Christianity is just one more religion. The resurrection declares that faith in Christ is a personal encounter with the living God, not just a philosophy, a set of morals, or the teachings of a spiritual leader. The resurrection declares the deity of Jesus Christ, God among us, all-powerful and triumphant over sin. It tells us that God came, took away our sins, and invited us to receive forgiveness.

In this study, we will focus our attention on what makes the resurrection so significant and what it means for us to fulfill the Great Commission.

The Gospel Accounts

1. The resurrection is recorded in all four Gospels: Matthew 28:1–15; Mark 16:1–14; Luke 24:1–49; John 20:1–31. What facts appear in all four of these accounts?

2. What do you gain from having four different accounts of this event?

The Significance of the Resurrection

3. What makes the resurrection significant to your faith (see 1 Corinthians 15:12–19)?

4. What implications does Christ's resurrection have for your understanding about life after death (see 1 Corinthians 15:29–32, 35–54)?

5. How does the resurrection give you hope?

6. How does Christ's death on the cross and his resurrection especially touch you?

The Great Commission

Remember when people used to ask you, "What do you want to be when you grow up?" Whatever your answer to that question was when you were younger, you probably had *some* reply. Even if you didn't have specific plans for the future, you knew that eventually you would become an adult. One day you would grow up.

To grow up is a mixed blessing. Adulthood brings new responsibilities as well as new opportunities. Not only can you do more, but you're also *expected* to do more. And like all change, adulthood brings you to more uncharted territory, making you unsure exactly what lies ahead. It's the same with being a Christian.

From among his many followers, Jesus chose twelve men to be with him all the time. It's true that he did this so they could learn for themselves, but there was another reason: so they could learn how to teach others. Jesus wanted his disciples not only to become godly men but also to become teachers of others. That meant, eventually, becoming disciple-makers themselves.

Jesus wants every Christian to mature to the point of making disciples. That means growing from a place of mere belief to that of persuading others to believe, helping new believers understand their faith, and encouraging other believers to follow Christ. In other words, following Jesus means passing on the faith to others—what is often called fulfilling the Great Commission.

The Call

The Scene: Imagine that you are the owner and president of a dynamic, medium-size company with about fifty employees. It's Tuesday night at about 8:30 p.m. You're sitting in your favorite living room chair. It's your first real moment today to rest and relax with your spouse. The workday is behind you, and the kids are in bed. Your cell phone rings, and you answer it . . .

You: Hello?

Caller: Hello, is _____ there?

You: Yes, this is _____.

Caller: Are you sitting down?

You: Well, as a matter of fact, I am.

Caller: That's good, because what I have to tell you may surprise you. This is the president of the United States.

You: Oh, sure it is . . . and I'm the queen of England! Come on, who is this really?

Caller: This is no prank call. This is your president, and I am very serious about this. If you don't believe me, just look out your front door. You will find two men standing there in dark suits. They are Secret Service agents, and they will show you IDs if necessary.

You: Okay, I'll check—and let me add, they had better be there. (*You go to the front door. Sure enough, two men in dark suits are standing there, just as the caller said. You ask for their IDs, and they show them. Suddenly, you realize you have been rude to the president of the United States! You put the phone back to your ear.*)

You: Mr. President, I'm sorry, really . . . I just never expected in a million years to hear from you!

President: I understand.

You: What can I do for you, sir?

President: Please listen. I have a matter of grave importance to communicate to you.

You: I'm all ears, Mr. President. Go ahead.

President: There is an issue of national security and world peace at stake, and, though you may find this hard to believe, you are the only one—let me repeat that, *the only one*—who can help. The future of our country and the world is hanging in the balance. I need you. We need you. The world needs you. Do you want me to continue?

You: Oh, yes, Mr. President, anything I can do for my country.

President: I am glad you are willing. I cannot stress enough that you are the only one we can count on.

You: I understand, Mr. President. What can I do?

President: We need you to go on a mission—a top-secret mission. You will not know where you are going until you are at the Air Force base awaiting takeoff.

You: It sounds very exciting, sir. Tell me more.

President: Well, there is one major catch, and as we see it, no way around it.

You: What's that, sir?

President: The mission will take ten years, during which time you will be completely unable to contact any friends or loved ones.

You: Wow! That is a catch!

President: We will give you one year to prepare yourself, your family, and your business for your absence. Your departure date is set for one year from today. I will have my people get in touch with you to help you in any way possible. Please plan carefully and thoughtfully, as you will have no contact with the life you now have for ten years. You will receive a packet of information shortly with all the necessary details. I will also call back to see how preparations are going. Until then, thank you. The world will perhaps never know just how significant a role you played in its destiny.

7. If you were this person, what are some things you would do in the one year you have been given to prepare for your departure?

8. What would you do to ensure the company you led maintained in your absence the same values, practices, and performance standards that are so important to you now?

How Jesus Made Disciples

9. *Jesus focused on a few.* How many disciples did Jesus train closely (see Mark 3:14–19)?

10. *Jesus selected them carefully.* How did Jesus choose the twelve with whom he worked closely (see Luke 6:12–13)?

11. *Jesus trained them.* Why did Jesus choose the Twelve (see Mark 3:13–14)? What purpose did he have in sending his disciples out to preach? What final mission did Jesus give his twelve disciples (see Matthew 28:18–20)?

Apply It to Your Life

12. What tasks does this "Great Commission" require of all Christians living today (see Matthew 28:18–20)?

13. How can your unique gifts and abilities be used in making disciples for Christ?

14. In what ways can you disciple your family?

15. In what way can you be a disciple-maker in your local church?

16. What coworkers, neighbors, or friends can you serve as Christ's messenger?

17. In what ways do you think discipling others will eventually impact the world?

18. What is one change you could make in your life to better fulfill Jesus' call to make disciples?

Your Walk with God

Bible

Schedule three times this week to be alone with God. Each day, read the passage indicated below and answer the questions that follow.

DAY ONE: ACTS 1:1–11

Some of the things I observe in this passage:

One idea for how to apply this passage to my life:

DAY TWO: ACTS 1:12–2:21

Some of the things I observe in this passage:

One idea for how to apply this passage to my life:

DAY THREE: ACTS 2:22–47

Some of the things I observe in this passage:

One idea for how to apply this passage to my life:

Prayer

On each of your three days with God this week, pray for the following:

Day One (Adoration): From your memory of all you've learned in this part of *The Way of a Disciple,* make a list of all the praiseworthy deeds that Jesus did as a man on earth. Praise him for his deeds.

Day Two (Confession). Ask God to bring to mind any sins of which you have not been aware, and confess these to him. Also ask God to forgive any hardness or insensitivity you may have had toward Christ.

Day Three (Supplication): Write out a prayer of devotion to Jesus, asking God to make you a better follower each day.

Scripture Memory

Memorize this verse this week.

> *Therefore, my dear brothers and sisters, stand firm. Let nothing move you. Always give yourselves fully to the work of the Lord, because you know that your labor in the Lord is not in vain* (1 Corinthians 15:58).

On Your Own: The Resurrection Story

Reading the different accounts of the resurrection may raise questions about why the Gospels differ in various details of the story. For example, you may wonder:

- Was there one angel or two?
- How many women went to the tomb?
- Were the angels outside or inside the tomb?
- Who actually went into the tomb?
- Did Peter go *into* the tomb or just *look* inside?

These kinds of questions may lead to deeper ones:

- Why didn't God cause the writers to report the details exactly alike? Isn't the Bible infallible and inerrant?
- How can we explain the apparent contradictions between the Gospels?

The following three principles may help you as you ponder such questions.

1. Each Writer Left Out Some Details

A true contradiction in the gospel accounts is actually harder to find than you might expect. For example, does John's comment in John 20:1—that Mary Magdalene went to the tomb, with no mention of any other women going with her—rule out the possibility that other women were with her but just not mentioned? Not at all. John's story doesn't really contradict the others; it just doesn't say everything.

We have a hint of this in John 20:2, where Mary says "we," so even in John's gospel, there's an implicit assertion that she was not alone. In other words, facts left out of one account but not another do not necessarily indicate a contradiction. A true contradiction would be a statement such as, "Mary Magdalene came early to the tomb alone—and no one was with her." No such contradictory statements exist in the Gospels.

Consider the following story. A woman was waiting for a bus with a friend. As the bus approached, the crowd pressed forward, and the woman was pushed into the path of the bus. The bus struck her, and an ambulance was called. The friend called the woman's husband and told him, "Your wife has been hit by a bus. Her injuries aren't severe. I'll call you when we find out which hospital she's been taken to."

About an hour later, the husband received another call. This time it was a police officer. "Sir," he said, "I'm sorry to inform you, but your wife has just been killed in a car accident." When the man expressed his shock because he had heard that her injuries from being hit by a bus were not severe, the officer replied that there was no bus involved. His wife had been killed while a passenger in an automobile.

From the looks of the above story, the stories of police officer and the friend contradict each other. Somebody is mistaken on which vehicles were involved and the nature of the woman's injuries (or one or both of those people called the wrong husband!). In any event, if we were reading this account in two different newspapers (one story from the officer and one from the friend), it would not be hard to assume the accounts were mixed up. After reading those stories, we would want to ask some questions to find out what really went on.

As it turns out, both the friend and the police officer were 100 percent correct in every detail. The woman had been hit by a bus. Before the ambulance arrived, a passerby offered to take her to the hospital. While en route in that car, the woman was involved in the fatal auto accident. The two stories could be completely harmonized, omitting nothing. Had someone tampered with either story to erase the contradiction, the final story would not have been true to the actual events. So leaving the stories as they are, even with apparent contradictions, is a more honest and credible option.

That is how the Gospels come to us. In many cases they actually complement each other without negating each other.

2. Differences Often Authenticate a Story

In fact, differences often authenticate a story because they prove there has been no attempt to change the details to harmonize the accounts. When faced with a possible contradiction, even generally honest people may fudge some of the details to make stories fit. This is especially true of dishonest people. But in the New Testament, we don't see such adjustments—the writers told their stories as they saw them (or heard them). And as we said above, the contradictions may not turn out to be real contradictions after all.

3. God Is Incapable of Falsehood

We say the Bible is "God-breathed" and without error because any book from God (as fulfilled prophecy and its incredible trustworthiness show that it is) would have to be utterly and completely truthful. God cannot lie, nor can he mix truth with error. And if God says something through a prophet, it will always and in every case be true, because God is speaking and he cannot speak falsely.

No prophet speaking by God's Spirit ever uttered a falsehood. "No prophecy of Scripture came about by the prophet's own interpretation of things. For prophecy never had its origin in the human will, but prophets, though human, spoke from God as they were carried along by the Holy Spirit" (2 Peter 1:20–21). Since the Scriptures are God's Word, they contain no errors.

What then should we do when we come upon an apparent contradiction or mistake? We recognize them as such and try to solve them. We harmonize the accounts or admit we don't know. But the one option we don't have is to impute error to God. Once we say that God inspired error, we open the door to anything in the Bible being a possible mistake.

If God ever told one lie, he could have told a thousand. But our God never has told us and never will tell us something that isn't true. That is why difficulties in Scripture don't change its inerrancy, because we anchor our hope of pure truth in his nature and recognize that such problems will ultimately have a solution.

Jesus had this view of Scripture. A quick survey of the Gospels will reveal his tremendous respect for its truth. Statements such as, "The scripture cannot be broken" (John 10:35 KJV) and "Since you do not believe what [Moses] wrote, how are you going to believe what I say?" (John 5:47), show Jesus' trust in and high view of the operation of God's Spirit in the Bible. If Jesus is Lord of our lives, then he is Lord of our beliefs; and he believed in the invulnerability and utter truthfulness of Scripture. So, to call him Lord is to agree with him about the nature of the Bible.

The accounts of Jesus' resurrection do differ. But their apparent contradictions are really just that—apparent. Our finite minds will have to wait for a full disclosure of details that will resolve all our questions. But based on who God is and in submission to the authority of Christ, we do not impute error to God, and we fully anticipate the answer to our every question that will show God's complete and eternal truthfulness.

FOLLOWING JESUS

This review is the culmination of your study of Part 3, "Following Jesus." Use this time to reflect on your experience and to summarize what you've learned about following Jesus. As you know by now, following Christ is more than just a matter of believing in Jesus. It is a personal relationship with him, involving prayer, worship, and trust. This review invites you to look back on what you've learned during this part of the study and apply it to that ongoing relationship.

Reflect on What You've Learned

1. During this part of the study, what has been your most meaningful insight about following Christ?

2. What does it mean to do everything to the glory of God?

3. What is one area of your life that you have submitted to the lordship of Christ as a result of this study?

4. What are some ways a Christian should serve Christ with money and possessions?

5. What are some benefits you receive as a result of following Jesus?

6. How have you had to adjust your expectations of God?

7. In what way does opposition to your faith challenge you?

8. What do you need to do to ready yourself for Jesus' return?

9. What about doing God's will do you find most difficult?

10. What is most meaningful to you about Christ's death?

11. Why is it significant that Jesus rose from the dead?

12. What can you do at this time in your life to help fulfill the Great Commission?

Self-Evaluation

Your group leader will be meeting with you to discuss your current spiritual condition and your hopes for growing in your faith. Please take some time to reflect honestly on where you stand right now within these four basic categories of Christian growth. Rate yourself in each category.

+ DOING WELL. I'M PLEASED WITH MY PROGRESS SO FAR.
x ON THE RIGHT TRACK, BUT I SEE DEFINITE AREAS FOR IMPROVEMENT.
− THIS IS A STRUGGLE. I NEED SOME HELP.

A Disciple Is One Who . . .

13. *Walks with God.* To what extent is my Bible study and prayer time adequate for helping me walk with God?

Rating: _____

Comments:

14. *Lives the Word.* To what extent is my mind filled with scriptural truths so that my actions and reactions show I am being transformed?

Rating: _____

Comments:

15. *Contributes to the work.* To what extent am I actively participating in the church with my time, talents, and treasures?

Rating: _____

Comments:

16. *Impacts the world.* To what extent am I impacting my world with a Christian witness and influence?

Rating: _____

Comments:

17. Other issues I would like to discuss with my small-group leader:

The Work of a Disciple

Living Like Jesus

Don Cousins and Judson Poling

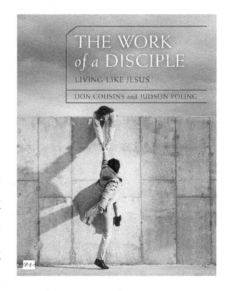

At its core, Christianity is not so much knowing about Jesus' teachings as it is about knowing him. As a believer in Christ, you embrace him as a person, not merely as a doctrine or philosophy. You form a relationship with the living God and become his disciples as you walk with him, live the Word, contribute to his work, and seek to impact your world.

The two volumes in the *Walking with God Series* have been written to help you and your small-group members put these practices into action and become disciples of Jesus. In this second volume, you will explore God's plan to connect his children in a life-sustaining community called the "church" and discover your place within it. You will examine how God made you and gifted you—not so he could merely *employ* you, but so you could experience the joy of being a co-builder of his kingdom. You will also look at how God called you to share the message of Christ with the world and how to make that happen.

Available in stores and online!